COMPELLED

COMPELLED

Nurturing Local Missional Communities:
A Pastoral Theology

KURT N. FREDRICKSON

Foreword by Tod Bolsinger

CASCADE *Books* • Eugene, Oregon

COMPELLED
Nurturing Local Missional Communities: A Pastoral Theology

Cascade Books
An Imprint of Wipf and Stock Publishers
199 W. 8th Ave., Suite 3
Eugene, OR 97401

www.wipfandstock.com

PAPERBACK ISBN: 979-8-3852-4009-8
HARDCOVER ISBN: 979-8-3852-4010-4
EBOOK ISBN: 979-8-3852-4011-1

Cataloguing-in-Publication data:

Names: Fredrickson, Kurt N., author. | Bolsinger, Tod, foreword.

Title: Compelled : Nurturing Local Missional Communities: A Pastoral Theology / Kurt N. Fredrickson; foreword by Tod Bolsinger.

Description: Eugene, OR: Cascade Books, 2026 | Includes bibliographical references and index.

Identifiers: ISBN 979-8-3852-4009-8 (paperback) | ISBN 979-8-3852-4010-4 (hardcover) | ISBN 979-8-3852-4011-1 (ebook)

Subjects: LCSH: Pastoral theology. | Missions—Theory. | Mission of the church.

Classification: BV4011.3 F38 2026 (paperback) | BV4011.3 (ebook)

VERSION NUMBER 05/01/26

Dedication

First Covenant Church, Oakland, California
The congregation and pastors who nurtured me in the faith.
I am grateful.

Simi Covenant Church, Simi Valley, California
The congregation I had the privilege of serving.
They encouraged my pastoral skills with love and patience.
I have been blessed.

My pastor-mentors: Stanley R. Henderson,
Werner Kroeker, John C. Notehelfer
These pastors modeled the way for me.

The staff, professors, and students
of the professional doctoral programs at Fuller Theological Seminary
You serve the church well day by day. It is an honor to work with you.

My family: Kristi, Lindsay, Daniel, Chris,
Malia, Nora, Cole, Quinn, Evan
These are the ones who sustain me and bring me joy.

Mission begins with a kind of explosion of joy. The news that the rejected and crucified Jesus is alive is something that cannot possibly be suppressed. It must be told. Who could be silent about such a fact? The mission of the Church in the pages of the New Testament is more like the fallout from a vast explosion, a radioactive fallout which is not lethal but life-giving.

—Lesslie Newbigin[1]

A church which pitches it tents without constantly looking out for new horizons, which does not continually strike camp, is being untrue to its calling. . . . [We must] play down our longing for certainty, accept what is risky, live by improvisation, and experiment.

—Hans Küng[2]

1. Newbigin, *Gospel in Pluralist Society*, 116.

2. Küng, *Church*, 130–31.

Contents

Foreword

I had just finished a morning in an idyllic community in the Scottish countryside introducing a sanctuary full of Church of Scotland pastors to the necessity of learning to lead in a dramatically and rapidly changing world. Indeed, when I first wrote *Canoeing the Mountains*, my genuine hope was to help pastors recognize that the world in which we were trained no longer exists. We were prepared for settled Christendom assumptions of church life, only to find ourselves "off the map" in uncharted territory. The call, I argued, was for adaptive leadership—leaders willing to face loss; learn in real time; and guide communities into an uncertain future with humility, resilience and hope.

As I walked into a lunch in the fellowship hall of that old Scottish church, an older pastor tapped me on the elbow to get my attention.

"I have one question that bothers me," he said.

I nodded for him to go on.

"I was trained as a minister. I am a minister. I am called to be a minister. But you keep calling me a 'leader.' I am not a leader; I am a minister."

My heart went out to him. I don't think he even realized how much his protestation was actually making my point. In the past, the focus of a pastoral calling was to minister the love of Christ to whomever was close at hand. To baptize, visit, lead worship, preach, and teach for those who came. To offer faithful service. (Indeed, we were all taught, to "minister" is to "serve.")

And while those tasks are still central to what pastors do, the changing world—even in rural Scotland—has meant that even more is required of us. The call to ministry means not only serving souls but leading congregations to faithful witness in places where so many have marginalized church life.

Indeed, pastoring is both ministry and leadership today.

Kurt Fredrickson's *Compelled* is a welcome resource for those pastors seeking to do this well. I, for one, am not surprised at all. For years I have worked with and even for Kurt as the associate dean of the doctor of ministry program where I teach. I have heard Kurt remind pastors that every bit of reading, every deep conversation, every lecture or project is more than just for making pastors smarter, but instead "fire for your ministry and oxygen for your soul."

This book is Kurt's tour de force. It is a book that both goads and grounds at the same time. Where my work sought to name the challenge and offer leadership practices for navigating a changing world, Kurt gives us a pastoral theology for thriving in it. This is not a book about ministerial self-care (as important as that is!) but about the pastoral calling as cultivating local missional communities for this new reality.

He begins with Ezekiel's haunting question, "Can these bones live?" and he answers with conviction: Yes—but only as pastors and congregations recover their "sent" identity, compelled not by success metrics or consumer expectations but by the love of Christ to cultivate a winsome—even compelling—way of life for those who don't realize for what they most are longing.

Kurt reminds us that ministry is more like tending a garden than running a machine. He helps us see that the task of the pastor is neither to prop up old systems nor to chase after the latest programmatic fix but to nurture a community that is formed in Christ for the sake of its neighborhood. In doing so, he adds a deeply pastoral dimension to the conversation about adaptive leadership. Change is not only about leading people but also about ministering to people: tending to their hearts, reorienting their imaginations, and modeling what it means to be compelled by love.

This is not an easy book—it is honest about the fatigue, the "low-grade fever" many pastors carry, and the costs of reorientation. But it is also hopeful. Kurt points us to the Spirit who breathes life into dry bones, to a vision of congregations who are more than religious consumers, and to the courage of leaders willing to be gardeners of God's mission.

For those who picked up the mantle of a new form of leadership but asked, "But what does it mean to be a minister in this world?"—this book is a gift and a guide.

TOD BOLSINGER
Founder, AE Sloan Leadership
Author of The Practicing Change Series

Acknowledgments

This book is a result of my lifelong vocation as a pastor, an administrator, and a teacher. I am grateful for the many people I have had the privilege of shepherding, leading, teaching, and serving. My life and my work have been enriched because of you.

My parents, Norman and Joyce Fredrickson, demonstrated a love for the church from my earliest days. They instilled in me a love for Jesus and his church. They devoted their lives to a local congregation. They encouraged and supported their pastors.

Special thanks to Dave Kludt, who was my first editor, serving as a compassionate critic. This book is so much better because of his work.

Introduction

"Can these bones live?" (Ezek 37:3). This is the question posed to the prophet Ezekiel in Ezek 37 during a difficult and tragic period in Israel's history. The people of Israel, captive in Babylon, were hopeless and weary, like dry bones, but the Lord offered a powerful word of hope. The Lord gave a promise to the people of Israel: "Prophesy to these bones and say to them, 'Dry bones, hear the word of the LORD! This is what the Sovereign LORD says to these bones: I will make breath enter you, and you will come to life. I will attach tendons to you and make flesh come upon you and cover you with skin; I will put breath in you, and you will come to life. Then you will know that I am the LORD'" (Ezek 37:4–6).

Can these bones live? Though in a very different context from Ezekiel, this same question is one congregations and ministry leaders ask. Ministry can be very challenging, agonizing even. At various seasons, it fills ministry leaders with a sense of dread. When the path is discouraging, when fruitfulness is difficult to see, when there is frustration or conflict, ministry leaders ask: Can the bones of this faith community live? Is there any hope? Can I keep going?

My wife and I were watching a movie about a man opening a new restaurant.[1] His life was consumed with the hassles of construction, health inspectors, animosity from the neighborhood, and staffing conflicts. These were matters mostly out of the owner's control. On opening night, it rains and the restaurant is almost completely empty. It is absolutely disheartening. As we watched the movie, I recalled how, on Sunday mornings in the middle of the first song, I would turn from my normal spot in the front row of our worship center and look back, wondering if the room was reasonably full or not. Sometimes I was happy; sometimes my heart sank. Sunday

1. Chbosky, *Nonnas*.

morning attendance was a key measure of a successful church and a key measure of my success as a pastor.

We had built this new worship center at our church. It was a beautiful space. Our congregation was thrilled to be in this new building. The building alone was a testimony to us that we were a thriving and successful congregation. But the building alone was not enough. We needed to fill this space Sunday after Sunday, and that was not happening as quickly as I wanted it to happen. I was under the illusion that people would show up just because the space was built. I was disappointed. Despite our great building, a new church just down the street with a much-sought-after pastor was attracting huge crowds. People from our congregation were switching to that church. This was a very tough season.

Can these bones live? Ministry life can feel like a valley of dry bones. The apostle Paul wrote about his ministry, "When we arrived in Macedonia, there was no rest for us. We faced conflict from every direction, with battles on the outside and fear on the inside" (2 Cor 7:5 NLT). This was my experience—conflict, battles, and fears—and the experience of many ministry leaders in various seasons of a vocational journey.

Can these bones live? In spite of it all, my answer is yes. Ministry and congregational life can be infused with life and vitality. The scattered dry bones can come together in a congregation. The breath of the Spirit can become a reality in a church filling it with a new sense of hope and promise. The mission remains. "Mission means serving, healing, and reconciling a divided, wounded humanity."[2] The local congregation can, should, play an important role in this mission.

A congregation can enter into new seasons of ministry as the people of God, the body of Christ, and the temple of the Spirit who worship together, conform to the image of Christ as disciples, care for each other, and witness in their neighborhood and beyond. Can these bones live? Yes, but the life a local congregation may look very different moving into the future than it has in the past.

You may be sensing the struggles that the apostle Paul did—conflicts on the outside, fear within (2 Cor 7:5). You may be asking the question for yourself and for your congregation: Can these bones live? I want to give you hope that the future can find you and your congregation in a time of renewal, with a fresh wind of the Spirit blowing. May this be your prayer of hope and confidence in the Lord:

2. Bosch, *Transforming Mission*, 505.

God breathe on us
in the valley of dry bones
in the midst of mourning
in the place of death

God breathe in us
on our dried up promises
on our abandoned dreams
on our unfilled hopes

God breathe through us
may your Spirit bring back hope
may your love renew your promises
may your work refresh and renew

Three in one, one in three
breathe on us; breathe in us; breathe through us
Fill us with resurrection life.

Amen.[3]

This is a tough and disruptive season to be a leader in ministry. The world is changing rapidly. The ways church used to be done do not get the same traction. For many reasons, the church has a new location in society; it is no longer at the center. Whether because of the distrust of institutions, clergy abuse, the pandemic, culture becoming more secular, or political divisions and unrest, pastors are waking up to the reality that they were trained to do ministry for a world that no longer exists. This is a difficult realization that can cause a good deal of anxiety. Kennon Callahan wrote decades ago, "The day of the professional minister is over. The day of the missionary pastor has come. . . . The day of the churched culture is over. The day of the mission field has come."[4] This is the new reality for ministry, and those of us who have been a part of church life for some time simply may not like it!

This changes the way we are church. This changes the way we do ministry. It calls into question many assumptions that were a part of being in ministry and doing church. This throws us off balance. It threatens our sense of value. It is unnerving. "The day of the missionary pastor has come. . . . The day of the mission field has come." This completely changes our

3. Sine, "God Breathe on Us."

4. Callahan, *Effective Church Leadership*, 3, 13.

orientation. And yet, this shift, though disruptive for a season, brings the promise of new life in a valley of dry bones.

As a pastor of a suburban congregation in Southern California for twenty-four years (the Evangelical Covenant Church of Simi Valley), I know the joys and the heartache of ministry. I have seen the church at its best and in some very trying moments. Church work is hard work. I know the struggles of transitioning a congregation through various stages of life. I know the despair of plans that do not produce the desired results. I know the frustration of others not grabbing onto the vision that seemed so clear to me. I know the pain of ambush and sabotage, both for me personally and for the mission that the congregation was pursuing. I know the discouragement of seeing some congregations in our community flourish (with seemingly little effort or in spite of themselves) while my ministry stumbled and sputtered. I have stretched the truth about my congregation at those pastors' meetings where others, along with me, are playing the ego-driven one-upping-the-other game. Sometimes I was fulfilled and overjoyed in my pastoral work. Other times, I felt nothing short of exhausted, demoralized, beaten up, beat down, and very alone.

In my role at Fuller Theological Seminary, overseeing the doctor of ministry and the doctor of global leadership programs, I have the opportunity to interact on a regular basis with pastors and other ministry leaders. I hear about their joys, breakthroughs, and their challenges. I hear their struggles and disappointments—with themselves, in their congregations. I hear their yearnings for the church to be more than it is today. I hear ministry leaders ask: Can these bones live?

All around the United States, we see glimpses of vigor: celebrity pastors, big church buildings, adrenaline-enriched worship experiences, and need-based programming attracting crowds. In the midst of this, ministry leaders so often ask: Why is my experience so different in the midst of all this seeming vitality?

I describe this questioning as a low-grade fever that infects church leaders. Most of the time, they don't acknowledge it. In fact, they often just try to ignore it. It is simply a low-grade fever. It is not enough of a fever to send someone to the urgent care, but it is a persistent fever. It is draining. It brings fatigue. And it won't go away. It nags at the pastor: "Church is to be more than this; my life is to be more than this." The fever is an underlying sense that church as it is in North America just isn't working. It is not having an impact, at least not as it once did. The role of the pastor in a congregation is questioned. Can these bones live? Can we jolt this body, my ministry, back to life?

In the midst of this climate of disruption and despair, and a sense of irrelevance of the church in a changing world, pastors and churches are often willing to do whatever it takes, seeking to infuse their congregation and their lives with ecclesiastical stimulants, hoping that the roar of the crowd will bring satisfaction and a sense of purpose. Pastors latch onto the latest surveys and techniques to capture broader audiences. Celebrity pastors are admired and emulated. Megachurch strategies are adopted as the next great idea or the last breath of a stagnant or dying congregation or ministry.

It is a low-grade fever. Or is it more than that? Frustration and body aches accompany the fever. Is this fever actually an indication that a congregation is in serious trouble? It might be a wake-up call so that ministry leaders might acknowledge the dis-ease and commit to listening to the Lord and to each other, thinking about ministry differently so that a new day of ministry might emerge.

One Monday morning some years ago, the Monday after Easter, I took a drive from my home in Simi Valley where I pastored to the Fuller bookstore in Pasadena. (What better way to unwind after Holy Week than to surround myself with books!) While I was on campus, I ran into a fellow Evangelical Covenant pastor. We asked each other how Easter went. I was tempted to give an answer about the energy of the services, the number of people who showed up, and on and on. But something inside of me said, "Tell the truth. For once, just tell the truth." I said to my friend, "Easter Sunday was a good day, but ministry is hard. I am struggling. Really struggling." My friend said, "Me too." For the next hour we shared with each other about our challenges, our doubts, and our yearnings. It helped for us both to realize that we were not alone in our struggles.

The fever is not readily spoken about. But when an opportunity is given, or when someone is vulnerable enough to say all is not well, church leaders begin to talk about the fever: about the changes in culture and ministry; about the sense of loss; about feelings of being in a cultural and ecclesial diaspora; and about fatigue, low morale, and a disheartening sense of ineffectiveness.

Church leaders and pastors want to serve well. There is a sense of call on their lives. They want to make a difference in the world. They did not step into this calling for fame or for financial gain. They believe that Jesus Christ and his church really can make a difference in lives, in a neighborhood, and in society. Reggie McNeal says, "This kind of call orders life around it. Personal ambitions and goals become subservient to it. The called live for a larger world than just themselves and their families."[5] Richard Carlson writes, "Simply put, 'call' concerns the questions and directions of 'what God wants me to do' and 'who God wants me to be.' Call is not my preference or profession or potential but my submission, service, and sacrifice. It's letting my life be led. 'A vocation takes you.'"[6] When God touches lives in this way, those who are called may say that there's nothing else they can do but serve the church in a pastoral role.

But there is this low-grade fever. It causes ministry leaders to question that call. All is not well. Can these bones live? Maybe pastors have this haunting feeling because they know that the markers commonly used to measure success or renewal are not the best indicators. Maybe business models, techniques, and strategic planning are not the ways to nurture a local faith community. Maybe pastors have a hunch that there is more—so much more—to church. Maybe pastors, nudged by the Spirit, are engaging in subversive thought, saying no to the predominant individualistic, consumerist, and entertainment-focused models for church.

I love the church, but I am not naïve about the church. Church has been a part of my life from my earliest days. I have seen the church at its best and in some of its more trying moments as well. It is "one part mystery, one part messy."[7] The church is the people of God, the body of Christ, and the temple of Spirit: that is mystery. The church is also ordinary people with issues and sometimes less than pure motives who come together as a particular congregation in a very concrete locality: that is messy. This church—one, holy, catholic, apostolic—is not perfect (often far from it). But, still, I believe in the church. I am not willing to give up on the church in its various forms.

Jesus has put us on mission. He said, "As the Father has sent me, so I am sending you" (John 20:21). This is the call upon the church, a local assembly of followers of Jesus. The church is a people who are sent on mission. At the core, this sending out as followers of Jesus offers life to a hurting world. It promises the transformation of people, of families, of congregations, of neighborhoods (and beyond) by the power of gospel of

5. McNeal, *Work of Heart*, 98.

6. Carlson, "Gift and Challenge," para. 7.

7. Eugene Peterson; quoted in Yancey, *Church: Why Bother?*, 45.

Jesus Christ. This transformation occurs because of the power of the Spirit at work. The apostle Paul writes,

> Therefore, if anyone is in Christ, the new creation has come: The old has gone, the new is here! All this is from God, who reconciled us to himself through Christ and gave us the ministry of reconciliation: that God was reconciling the world to himself in Christ, not counting people's sins against them. And he has committed to us the message of reconciliation. We are therefore Christ's ambassadors, as though God were making his appeal through us. We implore you on Christ's behalf: Be reconciled to God. (2 Cor 5:17–20)

The North American church exists in a transitional time. It is a time of chaos. This chaos should not lead to anarchy and the elimination of structure, nor should this chaos cause local congregations to abandon their history and traditions. Rather, in the midst of chaos, congregations can embrace the unpredictable and complex so that new missional structures and practices might emerge. New missional imaginations will bring vitality to local congregations.

This work of the church is ultimately the Lord's work and not ours. The Spirit of God is at work among the people of God. We work, but the Lord brings the harvest. Lesslie Newbigin writes, "Mission begins with a kind of explosion of joy . . . a [life-giving] radioactive fallout."[8] This is the work that ministry leaders are to do: calling people to new life in Christ that transforms people, churches, and neighborhoods while equipping a congregation to be a part of that endeavor. But because of the changed location of the church in the world, the way pastors engage in ministry must change. "The day of the missionary pastor has come. . . . The day of the mission field has come."[9]

Pastors and other ministry leaders are the ones who nurture a local congregation in worship, in discipleship, in care, and in witness. Paul spoke about being in labor until Christ is formed in people (Gal 4:19). These leaders play a key role in nurturing the missional tasks of a congregation. Pope Francis called this "pastoring in a missionary key."[10] This often happens in the very ordinariness of living: in the midst of the routines of a congregation, in both the best and the most challenging seasons.

8. Newbigin, *Gospel in Pluralist Society*, 116.

9. Callahan, *Effective Church Leadership*, 3, 13.

10. Francis, *Joy of the Gospel*, 21.

Pastors serve in this embodied space, working to form a people into Christ-likeness and encourage engagement beyond the church for the good of their neighborhood. Pastor and professor Eugene Peterson affirms the value of pastoral ministry. He writes,

> I've loved being a pastor, almost every minute of it. It's a difficult life because it's a demanding life. But the rewards are enormous—the rewards of being on the front line of seeing the gospel worked out in people's lives. I remain convinced that if you are called to it, being a pastor is the best life there is.[11]

Ministry leaders serve on the front line, seeing the gospel become a reality in the life of a congregation and neighborhood. It's the best life there is, but it's not easy.

A local congregation is more like a garden than a machine. There are no easy steps or strategic plans that will magically transform a church. There are no easy answers or methods. Congregational change is not a linear process. It is not a move from here to there, from point A to point B. Rather, a local congregation is provoked into fostering new environments where the Spirit of God can encourage people to become more like Jesus and imagine new ways of being church. As a congregation discerns its identity in a particular location, it will develop a deepening of the call to ministry within the congregation and in its neighborhood. Over time, a congregation can change its understandings of who it is in order to encourage fellow followers of Jesus and serve a changing world.

Ministry leaders often do this work with little or no recognition. It is lived out in very ordinary places, within normal routines. But it is essential, vital, and life changing. As Peterson writes, "The pervasive element in our two-thousand-year pastoral tradition is not someone who 'gets things done' but rather the person placed in the community to pay attention and call attention to 'what is going on right now' between men and women, with one another and with God—this kingdom of God that is primarily local, relentlessly personal, and prayerful 'without ceasing.'"[12]

> In one of his novels dealing with World War II, James Jones tells the story of a group of soldiers who took and held an obscure crossroads in France, shortly after the Normandy invasion. Most of them lost their lives in the effort, but the unit held its post until reinforcements arrived. Jones says that victory finally came in

11. Peterson, "Best Life," para. 6.

12. Peterson, *Pastor*, 5.

> the great war not so much because of the major battles that were fought and won but, rather, because of heroic skirmishes by a few people in a thousand obscure and out-of-the-way crossroads.[13]

This is the work of ministry leaders in local congregations. Most pastors will never get their names or stories written up in Christian magazines or blogs. But these ministry leaders on the front lines and at the crossroads are making a significant difference in the lives of people in neighborhoods and cities. This is the work ministry leaders do: not earth-shattering mission, but persistent, in season and out of season, work at local crossroads.

This work done by faithful pastors is driven by the compelling love of Christ. "For Christ's love compels us, because we are convinced that one died for all, and therefore all died. And he died for all, that those who live should no longer live for themselves but for him who died for them and was raised again" (2 Cor 5:14–15). This compelling love of Christ that transforms people, congregations, and neighborhoods is the driving motivation for why pastors do their work and, even more so, why they continue to serve even in the midst of challenges, internally and externally. The compelling love of Christ sustains the attentive work of ministry leaders.

The new ways of being church are not prescribed; the old ways are simply, sometimes painfully, disturbed so that something new might emerge.[14] Roman Catholic priest and missionary Vincent Donovan articulates the risk and the promise in the midst of gospel innovation:

> [This is a] movement not so much articulated in a book as acted out—something like a melody of a new unwritten song that haunts you, with the notes and the words not yet in place. It is there just out of your reach and the melody haunts you because it is not yet complete; a new song that many are trying to sing today. . . . You must have the courage to go with [people] to a place that neither you nor they have ever been. . . . When the gospel reaches a people where they are, their response to that gospel is the church in a new place, and the song they sing is that new, unsung song, that unwritten melody that haunts all of us.[15]

13. Willimon, "Rev. Parker's Last Stand," second to last para.

14. James Fowler puts it this way: "Pastoral care consists of all the ways a community of faith, under pastoral leadership, intentionally sponsors the awakening, shaping, rectifying, healing, and ongoing growth in vocation of Christian persons and community, under the pressure and power of the in-breaking kingdom of God" (*Faith Development*, loc. 140–41 of 1515).

15. Donovan, *Christianity Rediscovered*, xi.

Churches are not a relic of the past. Churches will continue to exist and even thrive in this new day. But the structures and practices of churches will change because of new cultural realities. A reimagined church emerging out of a new set of assumptions and practices requires repentance, a metanoia that calls the church to its knees, relinquishing past customs, methods, and structures, as well as its past privileged status.

In this book, I want to propose ideas that will help pastors reimagine what ministry leadership looks like in this age of change. Some of these ideas may be radical for the established church order. The role of clergy will change. Our metrics for assessing faithfulness and fruitfulness will change. Our polities and structures will change. There is some subversion here. But the discussion here will not be an either/or conversation. Rather, this will be an invitation to imagine how a local congregation can take steps, within the unique context, framework, and traditions of that church, to begin a journey toward a new way of being church. This will be disruptive. The reimagining will take a variety of forms in local contexts. This reimagining emerges out of a sense that the essence of Christian mission has been diluted along the way. Churches and ministry leaders have been caught up in and seduced by a celebrity-focused, consumer-oriented, entertainment-craving, crowd-pleasing, and shallow Christianity.

Change is never easy. Ministry leaders become anxious and tired along the way. The abandonment of old forms brings a sense of loss, anger, and sadness. Yet this torment of loss and dizziness can lead to new fires of missional imagination, resulting in new forms of church emerging that will impact the world for good, in the name of Jesus. Rather than just another new idea or program, what I propose is fostering a new mindset for nurturing communities of faith. It must be done slowly, with patience and discernment. And it should never be done alone.

This is the work of missional heretics helping the church imagine and innovate, while not letting go of the best of heritage and tradition. The word "heretic" may raise eyebrows and caution flags, but I use this term for just that reason. Heretics normally do not set out to destroy, rather to reform. They say things have to be different than they are. Ministry leaders must develop a missional understanding of church that is not a destructive disruption as much as it is a missional unsettling.[16]

Missional heretics are a vital component that disturbs the current ecclesial system and nurtures an ecclesial ecology capable of promoting

16. Terry Walling has written a great book on missional heretics: *Unlikely Nomads*.

new structures. Heretics scramble old categories. They are often unsettling and threatening, and they are necessary. The church must be characterized by a holy discontent marked by urgency and desire to move toward a holy madness. The church must not be content or simply give up. Ministry leaders must question, risk, and encourage others to question, and then church leaders must listen and act. Dutch missiologist Johannes Christiaan Hoekendijk once said, a bit tongue in cheek, that an awakened church that is authentic within the context of cultural diversity will have the following characteristics:

- It has developed its own way of sharing its faith in Jesus with other people.
- It is composing and singing its own songs.
- It conducts ecclesial life in a culturally appropriate, rather than exotic, manner.
- It manages to spawn a heresy or two.[17]

Heretics are intentional and curious. They face fear and refuse to back down. They say it is okay to experiment and even make some mistakes. Author Seth Godin writes,

> Heretics are engaged, passionate and more powerful and happier than everyone else. . . . Challenging the status quo requires a commitment, both public and private. It involves reaching out to others and putting your ideas on the line. . . . Heretics must believe. More than anyone else in the organization, it's the person who's challenging the status quo, the one who is daring to be great, who is truly present and not just punching the clock who must have the confidence of her beliefs.[18]

Missional leaders are ready to venture down new paths. Will we take the risk? Will we have the courage, because of the compelling love of Christ, to move out in new directions? Will we have the courage to step into a new day of ministry in new and fresh ways? Are you ready, willing, daring

17. Shenk, "Mission, Renewal," 158.

18. Godin, *Tribes*, 4. Seth Godin offers a delightful parable of a unicorn in a balloon factory. Balloon factory workers are very timid and fearful. They are afraid of needles, pins, and porcupines, anything sharp. Balloon factories are quiet and peaceful places of soft stability, until the unicorn shows up (72). Those who imagine missional change in churches and denominations are unicorns!

enough, aching enough, and compelled by love enough to imagine what a local congregation might become?

Ministry is practiced in the local, the concrete, the ordinary, and the routine. And yet something wonderful can happen in these mundane spaces. I will advocate for the significant role of pastors and other ministry leaders in that local context and at the same time disrupt commonly held views of how pastoral leaders live out their ministry. These changes for ministry leaders will impact people in the congregation, who will also be encouraged to view their lives and their pastors in a new way. Since pastors and other ministry leaders are at the forefront of ministry in local contexts, attention will be given to matters of the heart. Healthy, faithful, and fruitful congregations require health ministry leaders. This book will outline key elements for this nurturing of local missional communities:

> Chapter 1—Why: the why behind what we do. The forming of a missional congregation into Christ-likeness, Christoformity, is compelled by the love of Christ. This is a call to discipleship as a congregation worships, cares, disciples, and witnesses.
>
> Chapter 2—Where: the priority of the local congregation. This is where mission happens, on the ground, in concrete places, in neighborhoods.
>
> Chapter 3—Who: those who engage in ministry. This is a reorientation of the role of clergy. This is a call to embrace and encourage all followers of Jesus as those gifted and equipped to engage in mission within a congregation and outside the walls of a church.
>
> Chapter 4—How: an exploration of the frameworks, catalysts, and practices that provoke a congregation into a new missional posture.
>
> Chapter 5—Heart: nurturing a culture of goodness in a local congregation demands the heart health of ministry leaders and congregations. Ministry flows from the inside out.

The love of Christ compels us toward a new imagination for the church. This is a call to missional engagement in the world that will look radically different from the typical constructs of the church. This is our urgent task! Hans Küng writes, "A church which pitches its tents without constantly looking out for new horizons, which does not continually strike camp, is being untrue to its calling. . . . [We must] play down our longing for certainty, accept what is risky, live by improvisation, and experiment."[19] The task is still ours today. May this prayer be our prayer as we embark on this journey:

> Disturb us, Lord, when
> We are too well pleased with ourselves,
> When our dreams have come true
> Because we have dreamed too little,
> When we arrived safely
> Because we sailed too close to the shore.
>
> Disturb us, Lord, when
> With the abundance of things we possess
> We have lost our thirst
> For the waters of life;
> Having fallen in love with life,
> We have ceased to dream of eternity
> And in our efforts to build a new earth,
> We have allowed our vision
> Of the new Heaven to dim.
>
> Disturb us, Lord, to dare more boldly,
> To venture on wider seas
> Where storms will show your mastery;
> Where losing sight of land,
> We shall find the stars.
>
> We ask You to push back
> The horizons of our hopes;
> And to push into the future
> In strength, courage, hope, and love.[20]

Can these bones live? Yes!

19. Küng, *Church*, 130–31.

20. Addison H. Groff, "A Prayer for the Day," from *Minister's Manual* (1962); quoted in Keefe-Perry, "Disturb Us, O Lord."

1

Why

SETTLED OR SENT?

This is the question every church must ask, no matter what form or size or location. As congregations assemble as a local expression of the body of Christ, is this a gathering simply for those in that community, or is there also a focus outward toward others? This core question reveals the heart of a congregation and sets its path forward. Denominational leader Wes Granberg-Michaelson writes, "The missional church places its commitment to join in God's mission in the world at the heart of its life and identity."[1]

A congregation can be focused inwardly: circling the wagons, safe, protected from messiness and complexities, and concerned only with itself. This congregation certainly can be doing very good work, but it is muted, not living up to its full calling. A sent congregation is rooted in a location, worshipping, discipling, caring, while also demonstrating a sending attitude: looking out in new directions, willing to engage with the inconvenience and untidiness around them, and wondering how we might engage in their neighborhood witnessing the good news of the gospel in that concrete location. A sent congregation reveals an urgency about being good news, gospel people within their congregation and in their neighborhood.

We know congregations that are settled. It is a safe religious community that truly cares for those in the congregation but is mostly isolated,

1. Granberg-Michaelson, *Unexpected Destinations*, loc. 3550 of 3602.

happy with its own, and shut off from the wider, messier, more complicated world. There is a flurry of activity: Bible studies, potlucks, teas, children's programs, choirs, and softball teams. They gather for worship each week and hear inspirational messages. They might be like the barnyard geese who gathered to hear about the glories of flight but remained grounded. "They did not fly! For the corn was good, and the barnyard was secure!"[2] These are well-intentioned churches but simply not fulfilling their calling.

A sent orientation changes the focus of a congregation. Rather than living for itself, a congregation not only cares for those who are part of that fellowship but actively and intentionally extends itself toward others. A congregation makes this commitment to engage in the neighbor's good because of the good news of the gospel.[3] The apostle Paul writes, "For Christ's love compels us, because we are convinced that one died for all, and therefore all died. And he died for all, that those who live should no longer live for themselves but for him who died for them and was raised again" (2 Cor 5:15–15).

Every congregation is to be a sent congregation. Sometimes churches fall short of this, but this is to be the very DNA of every church. Bonhoeffer writes, "The church is only the church when it exists for others."[4] The gospel is good news to a hurting, broken world. The gospel offers life. The gospel offers a transformation, the process of becoming a new creation (2 Cor 5:17). How can we keep silent? We are called to be ambassadors of this good news (2 Cor 5:20). The good news of the gospel compels the church, and propels it, to not only be a caring congregation but also a congregation that extends itself—a sent people.

This sent-ness will look different for every congregation, but the local church is always a church on mission. Every local congregation must resist the temptation to simply settle. Hans Küng writes, "The Church is always and everywhere a living people, gathered together from the peoples of this world and journeying through the midst of time. The Church is essentially

2. This parable is frequently attributed to Søren Kierkegaard and, while not clearly found in his published works, is grounded in many themes of his writing.

3. Pietists spoke of their work being for God's glory and the neighbor's good. This phrase comes from Hermann Franke. Here is the missional drive of Pietists: "God's great river of grace runs close by, as close as our very breath and even closer. Stretching out our roots into that river, venturing upward and outward in faith and hope, may we bear the good fruit of God's love in the world, to God's glory and our neighbor's good" (Gehrz and Pattie, *Pietist Option*, 118).

4. Bonhoeffer, *Letters and Papers*, 282.

en route, on a journey, a pilgrimage. A Church which pitches its tents without looking out constantly for new horizons, which does not continually strike camp, is being untrue to its calling."[5]

THE MODERN AMERICAN CHURCH

The American church has lost its way. Churches easily fall into a state of comfort, focusing on the confines of a church community. The disruptions are minimal; the world is kept at arm's length. This is a safe, secure, known environment. Or, worse, the churches seduced by an individualistic, entertainment-oriented, consumerist bent.

All around the United States we see glimpses of seeming vitality: big church buildings, adrenaline-enriched worship experiences, and need-based programming. Too often the growth churches experience is a result of people leaving another congregation (because of a move to a new city or a dissatisfaction with the previous church or pastor).[6] Our American success has led to a domesticated and nominal faith. The seeming expansion of Christianity belies its actual decline. Institutional religion is becoming irrelevant and obsolete.

Lacking the instincts of a missionary, too many churches in America have appropriated professional techniques, entertainment gimmicks, or business models as the best way to communicate the gospel in a changing world (or simply to grow in numbers). Some have turned churches into franchises and corporate outposts. Pastors have become CEOs. Some have taken the measurements of the corporate world as the proper measurements for church. Pastors have become professionals, distanced from their people and drained of passion for the good news. Churches have lost their first love. Eugene Peterson comments on the Americanization of the congregation, "turning each congregation into a market for religious consumers, an ecclesiastical business run along the lines of advertising techniques, organizational flow charts, and energized by impressive motivational rhetoric."[7] So, the local congregation loses its mission. It moves to being settled. It happens slowly, often without us recognizing it. Peterson continues,

5. Küng, *Church*, 130.
6. Earls, "Church Switchers."
7. Peterson, *Pastor*, 112.

> By the time I arrived on the scene as a pastor, the American church had reinterpreted the worship of God as an activity for religious consumers. Entertainment, cheerleading, and manipulation were conspicuous in high places. American worship was conceived as a public-relations campaign for Jesus and the angels. Worship had been cheapened into a commodity marketed by using tried-and-true advertising techniques. If so-called worshippers didn't "get anything out of it," there had been no worship worth coming back for. Instead of calling people to worship God, pastors all over the country were inviting people to "have a worship experience." Worship was evaluated on the "consumer satisfaction scale" of one to ten.[8]

The congregation I served in Southern California was growing in numbers. I never asked where they were coming from. I was just glad they were a part of our church. For a time, my denomination celebrated the "twenty-five largest churches." I wanted to be one of those! And, eventually, we were. Did that feed my ego? Yes. Still, I had a gnawing dissatisfaction with my ministry, along with my life. I got caught up in the busyness of doing church. We were growing, but were we the type of the church the Lord wanted us to be? Did we make a difference? Did anyone care? Was church about something beyond just more people, more staff, more buildings, and more cash?

Then, these people who had flocked to our church in a matter of time left for the next "exciting" congregation. Like a new restaurant in town, our congregation had been replaced as the new and interesting place to be. It was the cycle of consumer church, and I was caught up in it. The exodus of people to the next church bruised me deeply.[9] For me, it brought on a good deal of self-doubt, and I wondered what was wrong with me as the pastor. For the congregation, along with some financial implications, people started murmuring and wondering what was wrong with their congregation (or their pastor). It was a difficult season, full of frustration, conflicting expectations, and dashed dreams.

We asked ourselves hard questions. If our church suddenly was no longer in our town, would anyone notice? And if they did notice that we

8. Peterson, *Pastor*, 254.

9. When I meet someone who goes to a booming church, I ask them if they have always attended that church. Often they reply that they are new to this booming congregation, having previously been part of another congregation. There is a good deal of church shifting going on! See Chandler, *Feeding the Flock*.

were gone, would people be happy, sad, or indifferent? Our answer: we didn't think many would have cared. Our church was just a building that people drove by as they lived their lives. And we were content being settled.

This period of self-doubt, congregational conflicts, and an exodus of people to another congregation with a popular pastor impacted me deeply. It was a crisis of ministry. This season was a wake-up call for me and for our congregation. It brought me to my knees and to the beginning of a new understanding of my ministry. This could have been the moment when I just decided to be done with pastoral ministry. Instead, there was a reorientation, a pivot. The focus of the church changed, but more than that, a change occurred inside of me. I wanted to become a more authentic follower of Christ, for no other reason than simply knowing this is what I was to be as a person before the Lord.

This change was taking place in my life and, therefore, the life of our congregation. We were seeking to change the way we lived out being a follower of Jesus: not with flash and dazzle or gimmicks, not by bullying people into hearing the gospel, and not with might but with a quiet and persistent desire to be the "aroma of Christ" (2 Cor 2) in our world. This was a new stance: welcoming and humble.

The realization of being a different type of congregation—a congregation that cared not only for each other but also for our city—happened over time. We wanted to be a church that made a difference, a congregation that served our community, and people that sought our neighbor's good. Could these bones live? Could we be a different type of congregation?

I began to change. This pivot caused me to pastor differently. For too long, my ministry had focused on what I could do and what I could accomplish. My indicators of success (or to use "ministerial language," fruitfulness) was bodies, baptisms, budgets, and buildings. This wasn't intentional, but on reflection it was true. I had a rather triumphal and arrogant sense of ministry. I wanted to succeed. I wanted to be known as "that pastor" who serves "that church" (maybe called "my church"). The process of reevaluating all this shook me to the core.

A new stance in life was emerging from deep within: a stance of weakness and humility rather than triumph.[10] I was seeking to become less

10. "For Paul the church is a living exegesis of the gospel of God. The church 'performs the gospel as a living commentary on it. . . . It lives the story, embodies the story, tells the story.' And it does so because, and inasmuch as, it participates in the life of the God—Father, Son, and Spirit—who is the source and the content of that gospel" (Gorman, *Becoming the Gospel*, 43).

prideful and less interested in results. I was becoming focused on how our congregation could be a people who worshiped God, cared for each other, grew as followers of Jesus in the very ordinariness of our lives, and were a witness to our community, blessing others in Jesus's name.

I made a conscious effort to engage in the world around me. I engaged in our city in very intentional ways. I wanted to model new paradigms of ministry for the rest of the staff and for the congregation as a whole, but most of all I simply wanted to be a different type of pastor. The love of Christ, the gospel, compelled me. I joined a local Rotary Club, which led to me becoming a police chaplain in my community. That opened up the door for me to serve on the city's gang and homelessness task forces and as a member of the local free clinic and the community foundation. I was an unofficial advisor for the chief of police, the city manager, and the mayor. My world, my connections, and even my influence spread beyond the walls of the church. The new people I encountered were people with whom a deep affection grew. They were not a "project." They became new friends! And good things were happening.

We as a congregation began to change. We had a new focus, with new commitments emerging in the congregation. The change happened slowly. We were seeking what the Lord wanted from us. We determined that we would not be a settled people but a sent people. We didn't yet have words to describe what was happening to us, nor did we have a plan for what we were becoming. We knew only that our congregation did not exist just for ourselves. We were called to serve our community, to be a source of good in our world. Our church as we knew it began to change. We intentionally began moving to a servant-based and community-focused ministry. We sought to be "servants of Jesus Christ for the sake of the world."

Our congregation took on a new shape and identity. We did not develop new programs: no "back-to-church Sundays," no Evangelism Explosion, no door-to-door outreach, no car shows, and no iPad giveaways on Easter. Rather, we were lifting up the idea that everyone in the congregation can be salt and light—a witness to the good news in the very places where they live (at work, at school, in their neighborhoods, as they shop, as they coach a team, anywhere). They could witness and impact the lives of others for good—not in a gospel-thumping sort of way—simply by living their lives as followers of Jesus. With this new focus, structures and measurements of effective ministry also changed. Ministry became about more than the number of bodies in attendance, the number of paid staff, the size of the budget, and the number of buildings on the church campus. A shift was occurring in our congregation. It was happening slowly and incrementally. My way of doing ministry changed. My focus changed. The mood of our congregation was changing.

Our congregation began holding a monthly meeting for all ministry volunteers and pastoral staff. At the meeting every month we passed out two awards: the Salt and Light Award and the Towel and Basin Award. The Salt and Light Award was simply a wooden base with a mounted salt shaker and a flashlight spray-painted silver. It was given monthly to a volunteer engaged in ministry outside of the walls of the church. The Towel and Basin Award was also a wooden base with a towel and small bowl attached, spray-painted gold. This was given to a volunteer who engaged in ministry within the congregation. We were attempting to show the broad nature of the mission of our congregation.

Theologian Douglas John Hall has written extensively on a *theologia cruxis* over against a *theologia gloria*.[11] A theology of glory is one of the most predominant themes in North American Christianity; it is so firmly rooted that there is rarely an awareness (much less a critique) of it. A theology of glory develops nicely alongside the consumerist bent of the North American church where people demand, and the church willingly provides, religious goods and services for the hungry spiritual consumer. German pastor and theologian Dietrich Bonhoeffer wrote about and embodied a theology of the cross. Following the crucified one, success looks very different. Formed in the likeness of the crucified one, all standards of success change.[12]

In line with this theology of the cross, our congregation began to view church in a new way. Even though we didn't yet have the language, this was *missio Dei*, the mission of God. The church is the people of God only because of God's prior action. "It is not the church that has a mission of salvation to fulfill to the world; it is the mission of the Son and the Spirit through the Father that includes the church, creating a church as it goes on its way."[13] God is a sending, missionary God. Mission is rooted in the character of God. The church participates in God's prior mission. Missiologist David Bosch notes,

> Mission is understood as being derived from the very nature of God. It is thus put in the context of the doctrine of the Trinity,

11. See, for example, Hall, "Ecclesia Crucis."
12. Bonhoeffer, *Ethics*, 77, 81.
13. Moltmann, *Church in the Spirit*, 64.

> not ecclesiology or soteriology. The classical doctrine of *missio Dei* as God the Father sending the Son, and God the Father and Son sending the Holy Spirit is expanded to include yet another movement: Father, Son, and Holy Spirit sending the church into the world.[14]

We were developing a new focus as a congregation. It took courage to stick to this new way of church as a sent people intentionally being formed into the image of Christ, caring for each other, and extending ourselves into our neighborhood.

This was not easy. There were consequences. People left our congregation. They felt church had become too difficult or demanding. They disagreed with our new emphasis or felt we were too welcoming. We were no longer trying to be as flashy as some churches. Everyone had their own reason, but many left. That impacted the budget. It impacted the volunteer pool. It caused people to ask hard questions: Who are we as a church? Are we in trouble? Are we failing? Are we dying? And, do we have the right pastor?

Ministry leaders can say, "We have new measures for faithfulness and fruitfulness." Critics can say that is just an excuse, a reframing to justify the change and the loss. Using the old metrics, we were in trouble. Could our people see that new metrics—not the metrics of the business world and typical evangelical churches—were now in play?

This was, again, a new crisis of ministry! Again, it was difficult, with self-doubt and frustration surfacing. Fortunately, I had good people around me—congregational leaders and fellow staff—who continued to encourage me and this new focus. Authors also helped me see a new way forward and that I was not the only crazy one![15]

As I reflect on how our congregation changed to this new conviction of sent-ness, I see that this new stance evolved from below. This was not a top-down directive, but rather, through a discerning look at Scripture and modeling a new orientation and new practices, we became a different church. Ministries are provoked and disturbed more than they are dictated.

The church is more like a garden than a machine. Ministry leaders nurture new environments for churches from which new missional

14. Bosch, *Transforming Mission*, 390.

15. These are some of the voices that have helped me: Dallas Willard, Brian McLaren, Alan Roxburgh, Howard Snyder, Michael Frost, Alan Hirsch, Scot McKnight, and David Fitch. Later, my conversation partners became much more diverse: Soong-Chan Rah, Dave Gibbons, Efrem Smith, Diana Butler Bass, Phyllis Tickle, Tony Jones, Mandy Smith, and Nadia Bolz-Weber.

structures for the church might emerge: an "ecclesial ecology."[16] Pastors must see their role more as gardeners than machine operators. Gardeners embrace the different seasons of life, and gardener-like pastors work to create good environments for growth and provide just the right catalysts that will cause new life to emerge. This is an ecological systems understanding that will allow new opportunities for the church to engage in wild, untamed mission. While remaining rooted in a neighborhood, the church can move from being a settled congregation to a sent congregation. As these sent elements become embedded in the life of a congregation, new forms of being on mission will emerge. Consider any living system that we would like to see grow: a loaf of bread, a flower garden, or a culture in a petri dish. What are the conditions necessary for the elements that are part of the system to thrive, grow, and multiply? We do not create a program to make bread rise, flowers sprout, or a microscopic organism mutate. Rather, we provide the right elements and the right environment so that something new might happen. We can apply this thinking to ecclesial structures. This is a living out of 1 Cor 3:5–9:

> What, after all, is Apollos? And what is Paul? Only servants, through whom you came to believe—as the Lord has assigned to each his task. I planted the seed, Apollos watered it, but God has been making it grow. So neither the one who plants nor the one who waters is anything, but only God, who makes things grow. The one who plants and the one who waters have one purpose, and they will each be rewarded according to their own labor. For we are co-workers in God's service; you are God's field, God's building.

THE CHURCH IN DIASPORA

The world is changing. This means that the way we are church has to change. The way we used to do church—and also the way people were trained to do ministry—is no longer fruitful. We must be the church, whatever forms it takes, in new ways. This is not always easy. Sometimes it is quite disturbing. Missiologist and pastor Alan Roxburgh highlights this disruption, this unraveling:

16. This is a phrase coined by Craig Dykstra of the Lilly Endowment (Bullock, "Developing Missional Agencies," 106).

1. Up to the 60s, the Euro-tribal churches experienced a period of significant flourishing and saw themselves at or near the center of North American society.
2. Beginning in the mid-1960s that period came to an abrupt halt. The unraveling had begun, and it produced increasing levels of anxiety. The churches engaged in more than fifty years of efforts at church growth, health, and renewal, all to get back to their normative location at the center of society.
3. God's disruptive, dislocating Spirit is continuing to call these churches on a journey. After these fifty-plus years of unraveling, people might be ready to hear the Spirit's voice in fresh ways.[17]

This can be difficult to imagine, especially with people who have been a part of church life all of their lives, but the world has changed. When people have been part of a congregation or church life for a long time, often they don't notice the culture shift that has occurred: attendance patterns have shifted and declined, more people identify as Nones (no religious preference), and more people identify as Dones (people who had significant roles in their church but are now tired, frustrated, and done). For long-time churchgoers, faithfully involved in a local congregation year after year, it may seem to be church as usual, but this is no longer the case.

The very location of the church in society is different. To be a sent people, local congregations and pastors must do the difficult work of developing a new awareness of the surrounding world. The church must respond to this shift. Alan Roxburgh notes this new location of the church. He writes,

> We are not in a contemporary or temporary "exile." Such language made sense to a generation that came to leadership in the 1970s, but for the generations that followed, this is not some strange exilic land. Exile language is tinged with the eventuality that there's a way back. In truth, there is no returning, no going back. We are in a new location, a land many people call home, and so the churches must ask very different questions. Exile questions about how to fix and make the church work again won't help us to discern the Spirit.[18]

When we think of exile, there is the sense that we will return home and be able to go back to the old and familiar ways. Diaspora clearly indicates

17. Roxburgh, *Joining God, Remaking Church*, 45.
18. Roxburgh, *Joining God, Remaking Church*, 28.

there is no going home, because home as we knew it no longer exists. The church as we have known it is becoming obsolete. The way we used to do life is gone, never to return. This is hard to accept when we continue to see thriving churches or when people abandon their smaller struggling churches and join a larger "successful" church.

As our contexts and societies change, the church must adapt so that the message might continue to be heard and Christ be followed. The apostle Peter reminds us of who we are and where we are located:

> But you are a chosen people, a royal priesthood, a holy nation, God's special possession, that you may declare the praises of him who called you out of darkness into his wonderful light. Once you were not a people, but now you are the people of God; once you had not received mercy, but now you have received mercy. Dear friends, I urge you, as foreigners and exiles, to abstain from sinful desires, which wage war against your soul. Live such good lives among the pagans that, though they accuse you of doing wrong, they may see your good deeds and glorify God on the day he visits us. (1 Pet 2:9–12)

The church in North America is in diaspora. As much as some would love to go back to the old ways, or to cling to the old ways, that is no longer possible. The message does not change, but the compelling love of Christ forces us to do ministry, to be the church, in new ways. Roxburgh offers important insights as we explore the state of the North American church in diaspora. He writes,

1. The missionary God who sends and participates in the world also sends the church into the world. The church is a living embodiment of this missionary God's identity and intention. This means everything the congregation does is shaped by a missionary commitment to the local context.

2. In our North American setting, the church is sent to engage and participate in our postmodern, post-Christendom, globalized contexts.

3. The church's internal life focuses on every believer living as a disciple engaging in mission. Worship, teaching, spiritual practice, fellowship—all are to prepare and send people to participate fully in God's mission.

4. If the church is not the primary actor, but God is, then we have to assume God is already ahead of us. The church embodies and

participates in what God is already doing. The questions "What is God doing?" and "Where is God doing it?" now have to form the practices of the church. The church cannot know how to embody the life of God unless it is alert to what God is already up to and participating with God in the specificity of its context.

5. The church's primary work is to listen for what God is already up to. Its life should be marked by listening, watching, entering, and participating in the life of the neighborhoods where God's people live in the ordinary and everyday, rather as Jesus did. "The Word came and dwelled (or 'pitched his tent') among us" (John 1:14).[19]

This signals a radical shifting of the ministry of the local church and casts a new imagination for how a church might be. The way we are to be the church changes, but the message—the beauty of the gospel—doesn't change. Here is how Tara Beth Leach says it:

> But the radiant gospel is about a people leaning into and reflecting the goodness of God to an embattled world. The radiant gospel is about the people of God in Christ extending the table and gathering as an alternative community in a world gone awry. We are to embody the power of blessing—that in the middle of a chaotic, prideful, sinful, decaying, embattled, broken world, we would embody the promises of Abraham and live the vision of Jesus as salt and light. As a covenant community in Christ, we don't just randomly do salt-and-light kind of things; rather, we are salt and light. As salt and light, we are called to mediate the goodness, light, love, and holiness of God. What a radiant call God has entrusted to God's people.[20]

We are a chosen people, in diaspora. The mission of the church, in every location and manifestation, is to awaken people to the message of the gospel, the reality of the reign of God. Missiologist David Bosch writes,

> The mission of God's people is to alert everyone everywhere to the universal reign of God through Christ. So everything that we do and say that alerts people to the fact that our God reigns through Christ is to be missional. So, it includes evangelism and personal witness. It will also include worship actually. But it also includes all the things that we do. In terms of active hospitality, of generosity and kindness and justice. So, a simple, off-the top-of-the-head

19. Roxburgh, *Joining God, Remaking Church*, 70–71.

20. Leach, *Radiant Church*, 26.

> definition is everything that we do that alerts others to the universal reign of God through Christ.[21]

The mission of the church continues as the church shares good news and people become faithful followers of Jesus. Locating the church in diaspora changes the way we do our work. The roles of clergy will change. Our metrics for effective and successful ministry will change. Our ecclesial structures will need to be reexamined. This is a necessity!

There is no doubt that this will be disruptive. The church must reimagine how it serves in this changing world. This can cause a good deal of anxiety in a local congregation. There will be a sense of loss, which can bring grief and anger. This requires a pastoral touch. People have memories attached to certain practices in church. A building holds memories of baptisms, weddings, and funerals. A hymn or song brings back memories of a meaningful time in life: a wedding, a funeral, giving your life to Christ. When certain spaces or activities are modified or eliminated, feelings are intensified. Pastors will be accused of not caring, not listening, or being insensitive. Ministry leaders must intentionally find the balance of nurturing a congregation forward and at the same time being sensitive to the feelings that change generates. Since the church is family, sisters and brothers, pastoral practices will have to engage a wide range of responses and feelings on this sent-ness journey.

Change is hard. Not doing ministry the way we have done church in the past is unsettling. We like our world, our lives, and our church the way it is. This will not always be easy. I don't like change. I don't like surprises. I like my old shoes, my favorite shirt, and my tattered jeans. I like the familiar and the comfortable. We like our churches the way they are. I like my church as it was! It is full of memories of good times and loved people.

Change brings anxiety. It simply is not comfortable. But the love of Christ compels us. We must step out into onto new paths. Our missionary God, the gospel itself, calls us to this. We are called off the map to do ministry in new ways. This is the task before us, but we are not the first to venture into new territories.

21. Bosch, *Believing in the Future*, 33.

THE CHURCH IN ANTIOCH

Every local church is called to be on mission, to be a sent people. Always. While that looks different for each congregation, no congregation can be content or merely turned inward. The book of Acts shows the activity of the Spirit, who is always pushing forward. The good news of Jesus cannot be contained or thwarted. The good news continues to advance. This is the mission of every congregation: sharing the good news, being formed into the image of Christ through worship, discipleship, and care, and blessing each other and the community in the name of Jesus. The church in Antioch, noted in the book of Acts, forges in new directions. This gives inspiration for the work we do today.

Author and former pastor Brian McLaren says the church today must exhibit not an Athens-based faith (where the message is domesticated and diluted by new cultures it encounters) or a Jerusalem-based faith (where the message is tamed and contained by a dominant culture from the past), but rather an Antioch-based faith where the gospel message never loses its wild, untamed essence; like a spring of living water or vibrant new wine, it always flows and is never contained by old forms.[22] Our model for church in this new season, in diaspora, is the church in Antioch.

This missionary church was not stuck in old conventions. It was willing to risk, to be stretched, and to be bold. They were a people called, gathered, and sent. This congregation began to view church in a new way: a courageous, risky way. "The church at Antioch became the crucible for the missional imagination of the Christian church."[23] The church in Antioch had a new lens, a new vision for what church was to be. Bevans and Schroeder write,

> Our contention over the last several years has been that it was here in Antioch that the church was born. We often speak of the day of Pentecost as the "birthday of the church," but we don't think this is true. We think it is here in Antioch, where the disciples were first called "Christians" (Acts 11: 26). Our reasoning is that before Antioch . . . the disciples saw themselves as Jews, not as members of a separate, discrete religion. Now . . . they began to see that in Jesus something new had begun, that God's mission in the world . . . had been handed over to them. And now they were called to continue this mission to the ends of the earth—in every nation,

22. Cited in R. Anderson, *Emergent Theology*, 5.

23. Granberg-Michaelson, *Unexpected Destinations*, loc. 2978–86 of 3602.

> in every culture, in every time period. Now it became clear . . . that God had chosen a particular people to carry on the divine mission, to be the face of the Spirit, the bodily presence of Jesus in the world. At Antioch and thereafter, what began to become clear is that God's mission has a church.[24]

In our contemporary world, the church exists in diaspora. We must reimage church.[25] Phyllis Tickle writes about the "great emergence": a sense that every five hundred years the church has a rummage sale. Tickle argues this occurred around AD 500 with Gregory the Great, in 1052 with the Great Schism, in 1517 with the Reformation, and it is happening again now. Her specific timing may be a bit rigid, but she makes a good and hope-filled point. In all times of transition, new forms of church emerge that are quite different from (and in reaction to) the norm. In this emergence, the older form of church is also renewed so that missional engagement now occurs from the renewed old form and an emerging new form.[26] Peter Drucker writes,

> Every few hundred years in Western society, there occurs a sharp transformation . . . within a few short decades, society rearranges itself—its worldview; its basic values; its social and political structure; its arts; its key institutions . . . fifty years later, there is a new world and the people born cannot even imagine the world in which their grandparents lived and into which their own parents were born. We are currently living in such a transformation.[27]

This missionally engaged church is not a specific form or structure. It is rather a mood, a missional vigor, that can pervade any church form—traditional or nontraditional, established or emerging. With the renewed thinking and practices, both the traditional church and emerging churches will be moved by the Spirit toward missional engagement.

The church must take on the characteristics of fire and gyroscope.[28] The church will be like fire as it moves from the orderly ways of a pendulum in a Swiss watch. Fire is a good metaphor for the wild and untamed church

24. Bevans and Schroeder, *Prophetic Dialogue*, loc. 356–64 of 3767.

25. See Fredrickson, "Ecclesial Ecology."

26. Tickle, *Great Emergence*. This neat and tidy five-hundred-year sense drives church historians crazy, but it does show that the church is not static.

27. Drucker, *Post-Capitalist Society*, 1.

28. Bergquist, *Postmodern Organization*, 4–8; Packard, "Organizational Structure, Religious Belief," 275–76. See also Kauffman, *At Home in Universe*.

that is emerging in traditional and nontraditional forms—as paradoxical as that might sound. Fire is irreversible. It consumes something and it cannot be reconstructed. Fire is ephemeral. It is all process and not much substance. It is more about becoming than being. Pendulums are predictable and reversible. Fire is not. Pendulum-type organizations (such as program-based churches) are mechanistic, solid, and reliable. They tend toward homeostasis (balance) and homeorhesis (the tendency to return to a common pathway or style). Fire-type organizations (such as missional and organic churches) are unpredictable, liquid, organic, and gravity defying. The fire organization exists, as Stuart Kauffman writes, between the highly ordered and the highly chaotic; it exists on the edge of order and chaos.[29]

A fire organization can also be described as a gyroscope: a gyroscope is a spinning wheel or disk that maintains orientation even as its axes spin freely in different directions. Gyroscopes are used primarily in navigation for maintaining a constant position of the traveling object relative to changing environmental conditions. The gyroscope fundamentally relies on movement to be effective; inertia causes the most distinctive feature of the gyroscope (the movement of the wheel around a freely moving axis) to give into other prevailing external forces, usually gravity.[30] We must press for change. Gerlach and Hine say, "The most effective response to a movement is another movement, for in times of rapid social change, survival lies not in stability but in flexibility, not in devotion to the past but in commitment to the future."[31]

The gospel demands this new orientation. The church has good news to share! Roland Allen, a century ago, imagined the spontaneous expansion of the church through the missional activity of the Spirit.[32] Emil Brunner writes, "The church exists by mission, just as fire exists by burning."[33] This is the church's primary identity and purpose. "To be a disciple of Jesus Christ and a member of his body is to live a missionary existence in the world."[34]

29. Bergquist, *Postmodern Organization*, 4–8.

30. Packard, "Organizational Structure, Religious Belief," 275–76.

31. Gerlach and Hine, *People, Power, Change*, 218.

32. Allen, *Spontaneous Expansion of Church.*

33. Shenk, *Write the Vision*, 87.

34. Shenk, *Write the Vision*, 90.

A NEW IMAGINATION FOR THE CHURCH

A shift in a church's focus is not easy. Sometimes the transition is very painful, even when it is a transition for the good. I believe in the church and, even more than before, I have great hope for the church, messy and full of mystery. Missiologist Charles Van Engen notes,

> When Jürgen Moltmann wrote *Hope for the Church*, he focused that hope in the local, believing community, proclaiming, "The local congregation is the future of the Church." He added: "God as love . . . can only be witnessed to and experienced in a congregation small enough for members to know each other and accept each other as they are accepted by Christ. The gospel of Christ crucified for us puts an end to religion as power and opens up the possibility of experiencing God in the context of genuine community as the God of love."[35]

The local congregation that gathers for worship, fellowship and care, witness, and service has the ability to impact lives and the world. Only the local church can do this. Missionary and missiologist Lesslie Newbigin reminds us that the local congregation is the "hermeneutic of the gospel"; the local congregation makes the gospel convincing:

> How is it possible that the gospel should be credible, that people should come to believe that the power which has the last word in human affairs is represented by a man hanging on a cross? I am suggesting that the only answer, the only hermeneutic of the gospel, is a congregation of men and women who believe it and live by it.[36]

Normal, ordinary people who dream big dreams and sometimes get caught up in conflicts. Ordinary people who sincerely desire to love God and others, but who also can forget to follow Jesus. Ordinary people, gathered in a local congregation, make the gospel credible for the world and serve the world! Who is able to do this task? Not us on our own, but only in the power of God. Paul reminds us, "But we have this treasure in jars of clay to show that this all-surpassing power is from God and not from us" (2 Cor 4:7).

35. Van Engen, *God's Missionary People*, 31–32.

36. Newbigin, *Gospel in Pluralist Society*, 227.

Church as Institution and Movement

For the local congregation to function well, it must operate as both an institution and a movement. Both are essential. This will require a new imagination for a local fellowship. The church requires the innovation of a movement and the stability of an institution. These must go hand in hand. This leads to what theologian L. Gregory Jones calls "traditioned innovation," where there are deep roots in orthodoxy and branches of innovation.[37] We appreciate and learn from our traditions as we move in new directions. Early Evangelical Covenant Church (often called Mission Friends) educator David Nyvall used a nautical image to illustrate this:

> On a well-equipped ship there is an anchor as well as sails. They both serve the welfare of the sailor, the anchor ensuring his conservation, his safety, the sail provided for his progress, including his goal, his home. The anchor does not mean rest, and the sails do not mean unrest. . . . I would hate to sail without an anchor, and certainly I cannot sail with the anchor alone. Sails and anchor are one in purpose, largely. Sails make the anchor very much needed, and the anchor makes the sails very much wanted.[38]

Institutions are organizations that seek to conserve the gains made by past social movements. Social movements are organizations that seek to call current institutions to make progress toward new gains. The church must operate with both in mind.

Decades ago, Ralph Winter, missiologist and founder of the US Center for World Mission (now Frontier Ventures), spoke of two forms God's redemptive mission in the world takes:

> On one hand the structure we call the New Testament church is a prototype of all subsequent Christian fellowships where old and young, male and female are gathered together as normal biological families in aggregate (a modality). On the other hand, Paul's missionary band can be considered a prototype of all subsequent missionary endeavors organized out of committed, experienced workers who affiliated themselves as a second decision beyond membership in the first structure (a sodality).[39]

37. See Duke Divinity School, "Traditioned Innovation Project"; Jones and Hogue, *Navigating the Future*.

38. P. Anderson, "Covenant and American Challenge," 139.

39. Winter, "God's Redemptive Mission," 122–23.

For Winter, the New Testament church in Jerusalem is like an institution. Paul's missionary band is like a movement. Winter sees these as two different ways of being on mission. I think this is a false dichotomy. It is not necessary to view the work of pastors and an entire congregation as either a modality or a sodality. Rather, the mission of a local church is to function as both a modality and a sodality. The church is a place of both caring and sending, worship and witness, in the context of community and discipleship. Pastors and other congregational leaders engage in efforts to equip and encourage both aspects. New Testament scholar Michael Gorman writes, "I think it is also appropriate, therefore, to use the terms 'centripetal' (moving toward a center) and 'centrifugal' (moving away from a center) to characterize this unified divine mission and the care of it by church leaders and communities."[40] When the church's mission is seen as including both of these aspects, the distinction between "pastoral" and "missional" action (or between "pastoral" and "evangelistic") collapses.[41]

The church in all of its local expressions is on mission. The local church embodies a sense of both institution and movement. And the local church's mission is always focused on the life of the congregation in worship, discipleship, and care, as well as focused on extension beyond itself in witness, forming new communities. Jesus calls us onto this mission. Brian McLaren writes, "I am a pro institution guy. I think institutions are tremendously important. I just think institutions constantly need movements knocking at the door to challenge them to take the next step forward."[42]

I advocate for the local church as a place of mission that involves aspects of both institution and movement. It is a group of people—messy, wonderful people—who are being formed into the image of Christ in local expressions of the people of God (the body of Christ, the temple of the Spirit). It is a local congregation (in many forms, in diaspora) on a missional journey of worship, discipleship, caring, witness, and sending.

Fuller professors Eddie Gibbs and Ryan Bolger, in their research on emerging churches in the UK and the US in the early 2000s, suggested nine patterns of new faith communities in postmodern cultures. While their focus was on new forms of church, these provide a glimpse into the attributes that might be incorporated into all churches on mission:

40. Gorman, *Becoming the Gospel*, 19.

41. Gorman, *Becoming the Gospel*, 40.

42. Tippett, "Brian McLaren." See also McLaren, *Great Spiritual Migration*.

1. Identify with the life of Jesus.
2. Transform the secular realm.
3. Live as community.
4. Welcome the stranger.
5. Serve with generosity.
6. Participate as producers.
7. Create as created beings.
8. Lead as a body.
9. Take part in spiritual activities.[43]

Here we find the creative edge of a different type of church. Gibbs and Bolger write, "Emerging churches are communities that follow Jesus and the kingdom into the far reaches of culture. Emerging churches destroy the Christendom idea that church is a place, a meeting, or a time. Church is a way of life, a rhythm, a community, a movement. Emerging churches dismantle all ideas of church that interfere with the work of the kingdom."[44] While I advocate more strongly for the importance of place and gathering for worship around the word and table, these attributes give but one glimpse into what local congregations might become with a renewed focus on being a sent people.

Church as Family

There must be no illusion. Church is a strange and wonderful gathering of people: called by God, united in the name of Jesus, by the power of the Spirit. The church—local and concrete—is always on mission, within the community of believers and beyond. This gathering of people is frequently referred to as siblings, sister and brothers in Christ. This is Paul's primary designation for followers of Jesus, used 271 times in the New Testament. New Testament scholar Scot McKnight notes that "the idea of siblingship is the dominant self-understanding and self-designation of the church."[45] This is where the work gets done. In very ordinary, routine, local churches.

43. Gibbs and Bolger, *Emerging Churches*. This list shapes the outline of the book, with a chapter discussing each of these nine points.

44. Gibbs and Bolger, *Emerging Churches*, 235.

45. McKnight, *Pastor Paul*, 61.

Church is family. We are on this road together. We laugh, we care, we cry, we worship, we are convicted, we are challenged, we are comforted, we get angry, and we serve. This is church: local, mystery and mess. And in the midst of it all we are being formed into the image of Christ, gathered and sent.

Being Formed in Christ

We are now getting to the very heart of the matter. The reason a congregation is driven to be a sent people is because of the good news of the gospel. The gospel of Jesus Christ makes a difference—the ultimate difference—in the lives of people. Paul exclaimed, "For I am not ashamed of this Good News about Christ. It is the power of God at work, saving everyone who believes" (Rom 1:16 NLT). This gospel changes everything, and so we are compelled to share it. The local church is a key way for that sharing to take place. This is the heart of the gospel message:

> And all of this is a gift from God, who brought us back to himself through Christ. And God has given us this task of reconciling people to him. For God was in Christ, reconciling the world to himself, no longer counting people's sins against them. And he gave us this wonderful message of reconciliation. So we are Christ's ambassadors. (2 Cor 5:18–20)

A sense of the church on mission, being ambassadors of Christ, moves a congregation beyond individualistic, consumer, and entertainment-oriented faith. Our concern is not getting a bigger crowd but developing people who follow Jesus as a congregation and in their lives. This is a call to discipleship—forming people into the image of Christ. This is the central focus of the work of a local congregation. The apostle Paul writes, "My dear children, for whom I am again in the pains of childbirth until Christ is formed in you" (Gal 4:19).

Michael Gorman uses the word "cruciformity"—following the way of the cross.[46] Gorman writes, "To put it simply: the cross of Christ reveals a missional, justifying, justice-making God and creates a missional, justified, justice-making people. Because the cross reveals a missional God, the church saved and shaped by the cross will be a missional people."[47] Scot

46. Gorman, *Cruciformity*.

47. Gorman, *Becoming the Gospel*, 9.

McKnight uses the word "Christoformity"—formed into the image of Christ. We are called to become like Christ in every aspect of our lives, including our lives together in our congregation. This is a life conforming to Christ, striving for unity and peace as sisters and brothers in Christ. McKnight writes,

> The way we become Christoform is through participation in Christ: through baptism, through faith, through indwelling and being indwelled by Christ, through the Spirit, through being clothed with Christ, through fellowship, through transformation, and through sharing all the events in Christ's life. Christoformity is rooted in Jesus's own words and life. Hence Jesus said, A disciple is not above the teacher, nor a slave above the master; it is enough for the disciple to be like the teacher, and the slave like the master. If they have called the master of the house Beelzebul, how much more will they malign those of his household! (Matt 10:24–25). For the Son of Man came not to be served but to serve, and to give his life a ransom for many (Mark 10:45).[48]

In *Evangelism After Christendom*, professor Bryan Stone summarizes his view on evangelism: "The thesis of this book is that the most evangelistic thing the church can do today is to be the church—to be formed imaginatively by the Holy Spirit through core practices such as worship, forgiveness, hospitality, and economic sharing into a distinctive people in the world, a new social option, the body of Christ."[49] This forming is not just for the purpose of witness, though that is true. This forming is at the very core of what it means to be church.

Living a christoformed or cruciformed life is a call to discipleship and mission.[50] This is the call on every congregation: to be a missional people of God gathered and sent, always being formed into the image of Christ. Yet, there is a disease that is inflicting American Christianity. Professor Kenda Creasy Dean calls the disease (and titles her book) "almost Christian." She quotes John Wesley: "The church is full of almost Christians who have not

48. McKnight, *Pastor Paul*, 4.

49. Stone, *Evangelism After Christendom*, 2.

50. Gorman writes, "Indeed, if 'salvation,' broadly understood, is the context and goal of all Christian activity, then in a fundamental sense the normal distinction between 'pastoral' and 'missional' action (and between 'pastoral' and 'evangelistic) collapses, since the ultimate good of the other is the focus of all action: entrance into or growth in the reality of God's project to save humanity. That is, for Paul all Christian praxis is inherently missional" (*Becoming the Gospel*, 40).

gone all the way with Christ." She similarly quotes George Whitefield: "An almost Christian chiefly is one that is fond of form, but never experiences the power of godliness in is heart."[51] We can no longer be content with an easy faith. To be a sent people, something has to change, down to the very core of how we imagine the church. This is a call to walk daily with Christ, to strive to surrender our lives—every aspect of our lives—to him.

We have settled for something less than what Jesus has called us to. The American church is trapped in an easy Christianity. This is what Dietrich Bonhoeffer called cheap grace:

> Cheap grace is the preaching of forgiveness without requiring repentance, baptism without church discipline, Communion without confession, absolution without personal confession. Cheap grace is grace without discipleship, grace without the cross, grace without Jesus Christ, living and incarnate.[52]

Church as fellowship is more than just a social gathering. It is an intentional and communal push toward Jesus. John Wesley's term is "consequential faith," a highly devoted faith, a faith that grows out of a desire to love God and others.[53] This type of faith has a sense of God gripping our lives, of getting caught up in a larger story that makes significant demands on our lives and offers hope for the world. More than anything else, this type of faith is all about cleaving to a person—to Jesus. It is a "white-hot faith"![54] In C. S. Lewis's terms, the church is to develop "little Christs": "The church exists for nothing else but to draw men into Christ, to make them little Christs. If they are not doing that, all the cathedrals, clergy, missions, sermons, even the Bible itself, are simply a waste of time. God became man for no other purpose."[55]

Professor Dallas Willard writes, "The greatest issue facing the world today, with all its heartbreaking needs, is whether those who, by profession or culture, are identified as 'Christians' will become disciples—students, apprentices, practitioners—of Jesus Christ, steadily learning from him how to live the life of the Kingdom of the Heavens into every corner of human existence."[56] He continues, "Most problems in contemporary churches

51. Creasy Dean, *Almost Christian*, loc. 25.
52. Bonhoeffer, *Cost of Discipleship*, 45.
53. Creasy Dean, *Almost Christian*, 5.
54. Addison, *Movements That Change World*, 41.
55. Lewis, *Mere Christianity*, 199.
56. Willard, *Great Omission*, 11.

can be explained by the fact that members have not yet decided to follow Christ."[57] This path of discipleship in local contexts creates a mood for the congregation.

This is the work of a local congregation. It shapes the culture of that local body to be devoted and maturing followers of Christ, and it drives that local body toward each other, and into the neighborhood and world in mission. The goal of a local congregation is: forming people (a congregation) into the image of Christ (discipleship), in the context of the local church (community) on mission (*missio* Dei). The local church is an ecology of care (moving people from sickness to healing), an ecology of transformation (moving people from immaturity to maturity), and an ecology of mission (moving people from being settled to being sent).

In the congregation I pastored, I found a place to grow in my walk with Christ, to serve, to enjoy rich friendships and a good social life, to be cared for in scary moments, and to be comforted in the face of illness and death. All of the wonderful and crazy parts of church move toward one goal: being formed into the image of Christ. It is a view from below. This sense of being formed is often quiet and subversive. It is not planned or organized. It is like a seed growing in a field.

> Jesus said: "This is what the kingdom of God is like. A man scatters seed on the ground. Night and day, whether he sleeps or gets up, the seed sprouts and grows, though he does not know how. All by itself the soil produces grain—first the stalk, then the head, then the full kernel in the head. As soon as the grain is ripe, he puts the sickle to it, because the harvest has come." (Mark 4:26–39)

Worship, preaching, Bible studies, small groups, teaching Sunday school, and going on mission trips all push toward this forming. But we are also pushed toward formation through softball leagues, women's teas, potlucks, church picnics and days at the beach, workdays, and even congregational meetings. As a congregation gathers and seeks to be formed into the image of Christ, slowly and silently people change; the congregation grows. It is all very ordinary and, sometimes, subversive.

Beneath the surface, the Lord is working. There is a subtext in every congregation. We need to learn to pay attention to the subtle workings of the Lord's Spirit. We need to learn to discern and pay attention to the routine aspects of a congregation: in times of celebration, heartache and

57. Willard, *Great Omission*, 15.

tragedy, and even in the moments of tension or criticism, trusting that the Lord is working in those times and places.

This sense of family, of siblings, maturing into the image of Christ first emerges from the stance of ministry leaders. Ministry leaders in a local congregation have the responsibility of shepherding the congregation in Christoformity (maturing in Christ) through worship, discipleship, caring, and witness.

> The pastor is called to nurture a culture of Christoformity . . . we are called to be conformed to Christ. Pastors are nurturers of Christoformity in this sense: we are formed by his life, by his death, and by his resurrection and ascension. We are not only to believe the gospel but also to embody it. . . . We become Christoform through participation in Christ: through baptism, through faith, through indwelling and being indwelled by Christ, through the Spirit, through being clothed with Christ, through fellowship, through transformation, and through sharing all the events in Christ's life.[58]

Pastors work to create a mood striving toward Christoformity with a spirit of humility, kindness, and generosity. Often it is unspoken, but there is a sense: Do we worship a gracious God or a stingy God? It shows up in all aspects of the life of a congregation. Often this is an unwritten curriculum. It is taught through the themes of sermons, the way pastors treat others, and even when there are disagreements. It is demonstrated in how pastors treat children, how pastors act in informal settings, and how pastors treat the marginalized. Do pastors keep eye contact with the person they are talking to, or are they scanning the crowd? Do pastors move through a crowd slowly or quickly? It is about developing relationships, nurturing people, and building a sense of trust.

Discipleship, being formed into the image of Christ, takes place in this local, concrete setting. The church is more—should be more—than an airport lounge. We are not merely spectators in the same room. We are sisters and brothers who worship, nurture, and witness together. We are specific people who are urging each other forward in the ways of Jesus. Every local congregation is on a path of discipleship. Being formed into the image of Christ is the driving force that propels a congregation into mission, both internally in worship, discipling, and care and externally in witness. A church becomes stagnant when it is not on this journey.

58. McKnight, *Pastor Paul*, 4.

In my congregation, being formed into the image of Christ became for us the intentional focus of our call as a congregation. This was our purpose that would be lived out in all that we did. This became the filter for what we did as a congregation. This would happen in overt, programmed ways. And even more so, this would occur in informal, spontaneous, relational, and ordinary ways. From worship, Sunday school, youth group gatherings, and Bible studies to meetings and service events. Everything! We saw that potlucks and church softball leagues were all, or at least could be, opportunities for formation. Ministry leaders were developing a lens that saw intentional interactions and informal conversations as opportunities for helping people on the Christ-formation journey.

> The church is the crucible that makes us disciples, the furnace that burns away selfishness and self-preference and every notion of a life of self-fulfillment and forges a purity of faith that is an affront to a world intoxicated with the self. I should add: the church is the crucible that makes us disciples if we will let it. And sometimes the only way we can let it make us disciples is to stay when we want to bolt. Or maybe I should say it this way: if you're not being inconvenienced regularly in church, you're probably doing it wrong.[59]

BEING A PIETIST—THE JOURNEY OF SPIRITUAL FORMATION

Pietism is my faith background and the tradition of my faith home, the Evangelical Covenant Church.[60] The Pietists in Northern Europe (those who would become, among other groups, the Evangelical Covenant Church) understood what it meant to be formed into the image of Christ. They were simple people who read the Bible and discovered, apart from the state church, new life in Christ. They called themselves Mission Friends: friends in Christ committed to each other and to mission. As they met each other or gathered in small groups, called conventicles, they would ask two questions: Are you alive in Jesus? How is your walk with the Lord?

Traditions approach conversion differently. The revival stream asks the question: When did you become a Christian? The Pietist stream asks: Are you still walking with Jesus? The first stream looks back toward the

59. Grothe, *Power of Place*, 179.

60. See Gehrz and Pattie, *Pietist Option*; Clifton-Soderstrom, *Angels, Worms, and Bogeys*.

moment when you became a Christian. The second stream is more concerned with today, this moment. Are you alive in Jesus now? Are you seeking to be his follower now? Are you abiding in him? It is a call to ongoing discipleship.

Conversion is not just a past event.[61] It is an ongoing journey. We become new people, changed people in Christ. And we live that out over a lifetime. The Pietistic tradition does not passively find assurance in a past instance of conversion. Pietism expects that the Spirit of Christ will work in the life of a follower of Jesus and transform that person into his image in an ongoing basis. And that transformation will be visible to others!

The church, the local church, is to be a people on mission, for God's glory and our neighbor's good. The church worships, cares, and encourages a faith that impacts all of life. This is the journey of discipleship. It is a lifelong task. Paul reminds us, "So then, just as you received Christ Jesus as Lord, continue to live your lives in him, rooted and built up in him, strengthened in the faith as you were taught, and overflowing with thankfulness" (Col 2:6–7).

Settled or sent? Every local congregation in its own unique way is to be a congregation on mission. Sent. Local congregations are called to mission as those who are being formed into the image of Christ. Granberg-Michaelson reflects on what Pat Kiefert calls the four movements in the life of those who become part of the body of Christ:

> That's where Jesus leads, that's what the Spirit empowers, and this is what God intends. The first three movements—calling, gathering, and centering—lead to the fourth, sending. At least that's the design. Joining in God's mission in the world is not an option just for some, or a program to carry out, or simply an annual trip to dig wells in Zambia. It's the expected outcome of hearing the call to follow Jesus, and responding. All this is the foundation for becoming a missional church.[62]

Called, gathered, centered, and sent. This is the journey of a person in a congregation. Become a follower of Jesus. Join with others in a community of faith. Grow in your relationship with Christ as people are cared for, nurtured, and discipled. And then venture out for the good of your neighbors. As we will explore in the next chapter, it happens locally and

61. See Peace, *Conversion in New Testament.*

62. Granberg-Michaelson, *Unexpected Destinations*, loc. 3437 of 3602.

concretely. It happens in a social context: relationally, intentionally, and also in the ordinary, commonplace moments of life together.

2

Where

The church is always local. No matter its shape or form, the church is an assembly of the people of God, the body of Christ, and the temple of the Spirit. The church exists in the world—the neighborhood—but is separate as well. Theologian and pastor Dietrich Bonhoeffer writes, "The disciples of Jesus must not fondly imagine that they can simply run away from the world and huddle together in a little band."[1] Missiologist David Bosch notes, "The church can be missionary only if its being-in-the-world is, at the same time, a being-different-from-the-world."[2]

When thinking about the mission of the church, the local church has three foci: worship, community, and witness. Professor Scott Sunquist reminds us, "The church, the body of Christ, has two basic purposes for its existence: worship and witness. All other functions point to and should aid in fulfilling these two purposes. . . . As a healthy organism breathes in and breathes out, so the church goes out in mission and returns to receive needed oxygen in community worship."[3] The church as community engages in worship and witness.

1. Bonhoeffer, *Cost of Discipleship*, 191.

2. Bosch, *Transforming Mission*, 386.

3. Sunquist, *Understanding Christian Mission*, 281. Newbigin sees the local congregation as the dominant location for which "the reality of the new creation is present, known, and experienced," and primarily for the sake of mission (Sunquist and Yong, *Gospel and Pluralism Today*, 111.)

The church, a local congregation, is a sacramental presence in the world.[4] It is all very earthy, and yet, something sacred happens in and through the people of God. Jesus understood the church's missional task in the language of call and obedience. The church is a sacred and sacramental people who are called out and sent into the world. "As you sent me into the world, I am sending them into the world" (John 17:18). "As the Father has sent me, I am sending you" (John 20:21). The church is the continuation of the mission of Jesus.

The church called out as a sacred people, now living out its story in obedience in the world, offers the world a gift. This sacramental presence is threaded from the call upon Abraham, to Israel, and then through Jesus to the church. As with the Jewish people through biblical and contemporary history, the church speaks bilingually. It first of all speaks the language of the biblical narrative, and then it must also speak the language of its context. This is the act of sacramental presence. The transformative power of God, which blesses the world, is given to the world.[5] We move into the neighborhood. The church is salt and light. It is a force for good in Jesus's name. We exist for the good of those within the community of faith and also those in the neighborhood.

We understand the church to be universal and global, existing for over two millennia. David Bosch writes, "The church-in-mission is, primarily, the local church everywhere in the world."[6] The church as the incarnating body of Christ must be engaged in the world. The church by its very nature cannot be separate from the world but rather is intimately involved in the world through mission. The church cannot abandon its mission, for in that abandonment the church would cease to exist.

The church, a local congregation, cannot be settled. It exists to be a sent people. The church has the obligation to stand against powers in order to do good and bring light. A local church cannot be silent. Bonhoeffer says, "The only way to follow Jesus is by living in the world. It is proclaiming a discipleship which liberates human beings from man-made dogmas, from burdens and oppressions, and from every anxiety and torture."[7]

These local gatherings are a people on mission. As Lesslie Newbigin says, "The church lives in the midst of history as a sign, instrument and

4. See Fredrickson, "Ecclesial Ecology."

5. J. Smith, *Introducing Radical Orthodoxy*, 238.

6. Bosch, *Transforming Mission*, 378.

7. Bonhoeffer, *Cost of Discipleship*, 48.

foretaste of the reign of God."[8] As a sign, the church points toward the kingdom in its fullness, through the ordinary work of people joined together in Christ. As an instrument, the church by the power of the Spirit works to make the kingdom a reality. As a foretaste, the local congregation, with all of its quirkiness, lives out in imperfect ways what it means to be followers of Jesus. The local church never exists just for itself.

The church we know is on the ground, a local congregation. Local churches are a mystery, and they are messy. On the one hand they are a mystery: the people of God, the body of Christ, the temple of the Spirit, formed in the mind of God from before time (Eph 1:1–5; Col 1:15–19). On the other hand, congregations are quite earthbound. They are messy: regular, quirky, wonderfully diverse people.

Congregations are a theological and a sociological reality. To the social scientist, the church is a human institution, subject to common and measurable forces. On the other hand, the theologian uses grand phrases to describe the church, noble aspirations into which a congregation should live. Both points of view are true, and we see the tension in ourselves every day. Jesuit priest and theologian Avery Dulles notes,

> To the Christian believer, the church is not a purely human thing; it is not simply of this creation or of this world; rather, it is the work of God who is present and operative in the Church through the Holy Spirit, in whom Christ continues his saving presence. Sociologically, the Church is a fact of observation, accessible to persons who do not have faith. Theologically, the Church is the mystery of grace, not knowable independently of faith.[9]

The local congregation consists of real people gathered in unique local spaces. Eugene Peterson writes, "Church is the appointed gathering of named people in particular places who practice a life of resurrection in a world in which death gets the biggest headlines."[10] McKnight calls the church a "fellowship of differents."[11] Pastor Dave Gibbons calls the church "a home for the misfits."[12]

Churches are made up of an ordinary, diverse group of humans, and every congregation is unique. Every congregation needs to be appreciated

8. Newbigin, *Open Secret*, 110.
9. Dulles, *Models of the Church*, 114.
10. Peterson, *Practice Resurrection*, 21.
11. McKnight, *Fellowship of Differents.*
12. Gibbons, *Small Cloud Rising.*

for who they are. As students in Fuller's doctor of ministry program write about the ministry challenges they face, we urge them to do in-depth studies of their ministry context. This exploration includes an understanding of the history of their congregation. What are the significant events and milestones, good and challenging, in the life of the church? Who are the key leaders, influencers, ministers, and laypeople? What are the demographics of the congregation? Where is the congregation located? What are the unique challenges facing the congregation because of where it is situated? In order to serve a congregation or a ministry well, ministry leaders need to have a good grasp of their context.

Churches exist in many shapes and forms. There is no ideal church. There is only the church in its embodied form: congregations of sometimes broken, sometimes beautiful saints. Eugene Peterson reminds us of this:

> People who made up my congregation had plenty of problems and more than enough inadequacies, but congregation is not defined by its collective problems. Congregation is a company of people who are defined by their creation in the image of God, living souls, whether they know it or not. They are not problems to be fixed, but mysteries to be honored and revered. Who else in the community other than the pastor has the assigned task of greeting men and women and welcoming them into a congregation in which they are known not by what is wrong with them, but by who they are, just as they are?[13]

These worshiping, witnessing people in community are just ordinary people, with hopes and dreams, failures and successes, and victories and disappointments. It is these real people who are the church on mission—in worship and discipleship, in sacrificial service, caring for those within the congregation, and witness—living for their neighbors' good. It is right here, at this very common level, that the congregation is the church and does the work of the gospel. Peterson notes,

> [Those in the church in North America] are the ones who do the un-heroic, routine things like showing up on Sundays, paying the bills, harassing their pastors, saying their prayers, hoping for heaven, and, more often than not, trying to be decent to those more and less fortunate than themselves. And in the midst of muddling through, there is occasional ecstasy, occasional heroism, the occasional act of self-surrendering love. It is all very human, and any

13. Peterson, *Pastor*, 137.

> serious conversation about Church and ministry must begin at that very human level.[14]

Father Richard John Neuhaus reminds us, "Our ministries can help transform the Church and help the Church transform the world. But we must be sure that it is the Church that we are talking about: the Church in all its thus and so-ness, in all its contradictions and compromises, in its circus of superficiality and moments of splendor."[15]

On my best days, as I participate in my local congregation—in worship or in an informal gathering—I marvel at this assembly of people. Here are regular, wonderful people gathered together in the name of Jesus. I listen to them sing. It is a beautiful chorus. I watch as people listen and are moved by a sermon. I notice the joy of people at a baptism service. I am stirred as people share in the Lord's Supper: "This is my body, my blood, for you, for all of you." It is all ordinary. And wonderful. Most congregations are not flashy. What makes a congregation vibrant are not adrenaline-enriched experiences but rather the quiet, gentle movement of the Spirit among a gathered group of people committed to Christ, each other, and the mission at hand. These "sent" congregations are alive with the gospel.

This tension between the ideal church and the real congregation, between the magnificent and the mundane, has always been the story of the church. The human and the divine aspects of the church are held in tension. The church is a sociological reality. We organize, program the church. And the church is also a creation of the Spirit. It is bigger than anything we could ever do. We must not overemphasize the sociological, assuming that we can create the church. Nor must we overemphasize God's working in the church thinking that we have no responsibility. We are caught between being fast-asleep churches (self-satisfied) or frenetic churches (frantically enacting programs).[16]

This local concrete gathering is often not easy. People are messy. We all are. And when we gather as church, there are bound to be times of disagreement. Sometimes those disagreements are trivial in retrospect. Other times

14. Neuhaus, *Freedom for Ministry*, 5.

15. Neuhaus, *Freedom for Ministry*, 9.

16. Hauerwas and Willimon further note, "The *fast-asleep church* is the self-satisfied church that boringly recycles habits and ways of the past without attending to changing social circumstances or to the machinations of the Holy Spirit. . . . The *frenetic church* frantically enacts programs to arrest decline and restore the church's lost social status, perhaps even making the church once again politically powerful" (*Holy Spirit*, 44–45; emphasis in original). See also Pickard, *Seeking the Church*, 210–225.

those differences cause great pain, disruption, and even withdrawal from one another. You might have heard the Gloria and Bill Gaither chorus:

> I'm so glad I'm a part of the family of God—
> I've been washed in the fountain, cleansed by His blood!
> Joint heirs with Jesus as we travel this sod,
> For I'm part of the family, the family of God.

These words speak of the wonder of the church gathered, the church as people joined to the Lord and to each other. It is a beautiful picture. You might also know this poem:

> To live above with the saints we love,
> Oh that will be wonder and glory.
> But to live below, with the saints we know,
> Well, that's another story.[17]

Something amazing happens as a local people gather, but it is not always easy!

The gathering of God's people must never be taken for granted. A local people makes a difference. I'm reminded of these words: "Do your little bit of good where you are; it's those little bits of good put together that overwhelm the world."[18] Rachel Held Evans says, "Church is a moment in time when the kingdom of God draws near, when a meal, a story, a song, an apology, and even a failure is made holy by the presence of Jesus among us, and within us."[19] The gathered people of God is a wonderful thing!

And yet, the gathered people of God can be quite frustrating, fickle, and exasperating for ministry leaders. I served as a pastor in a local congregation for nearly a quarter of a century. I loved being a pastor there, most of the time. Most of the time! There were times when being a pastor was very hard. Situations were difficult; people were troubling. I carried the burdens and the heartaches of many. At times, I was frustrated by the lack of commitment from others. Other times, I was discouraged because the congregation was not growing as I hoped it would.

17. Quoted in Davey, "Reconciliable Differences," 2. No one seems to know who actually wrote the poem, which is sometimes called an "Irish ditty" and sometimes is said to have originated in the 1920s.

18. These words are widely attributed to Desmond Tutu, likely from speeches or conversations but without a clear written and published source.

19. Evans, *Searching for Sunday*, 131.

But overall, there were many moments of profound joy and fulfillment. Lives were being impacted for the good. I was invited into the most sacred times of people's lives. The congregation celebrated the goodness of God together. The congregation cared for each other. Our church made a difference in our neighborhood and our world.

It is easy to either become very cynical about a local congregation or to idealize it, overlooking or burying the tough times. I look back on my time as a pastor with a keen sense of the joys and the challenges. I look back recognizing that it was a gift to serve this congregation. I loved the people in our congregation. And my family and I sensed the love and care of these people.

A THEOLOGY OF THE LOCAL CHURCH

The Church Is the Worshipping People of God.

The church, every local congregation, is the called-out people of God. The church is the pilgrim people of God. This is the church's primary identity. This identity drives the church in mission. It arises out of a shared history and a common memory. The concept of *missio Dei* informs our understanding of God in relationship to culture. The church's mission emerges out of the mission of God to the world. Ray Anderson writes, "Mission precedes and creates the church. Mission is the praxis of God through the power and presence of the Spirit of Christ. As a result of this mission, the church comes into being as the sign of the kingdom of God in the world."[20] "The mission of the church is fundamentally the *missio Dei*, the triune God's mission to reconcile and renew all creation."[21] Jesus gives this missional call upon the new people, the new community that he is forming:

> I am coming to you now, but I say these things while I am still in the world, so that they may have the full measure of my joy within them. I have given them your word and the world has hated them, for they are not of the world any more than I am of the world. My prayer is not that you take them out of the world but that you protect them from the evil one. They are not of the world, even as I am not of it. Sanctify them by the truth; your word is truth.

20. R. Anderson, *Shape of Practical Theology*, 30–31.

21. Van Gelder, *Missional Church and Denominations*, 148.

> As you sent me into the world, I have sent them into the world. For them I sanctify myself, that they too may be truly sanctified. (John 17:13–19)

A local congregation is not just a group of people gathered. It is so much more! The church's sense of election, of being a called-out people, emerges from an understanding of the language of the biblical narrative and the church's missional context. From the sense of election, the church lives out its apostolic and sacramental life of obedience. In obedient service, the church seeks to imitate the ways of God. The church is a foretaste of that kingdom. God calls the church, every congregation, to be "the bearer of his gospel."[22] A sense of election and vocation for the people of Israel emerges out of the call upon Abraham:

> Then the LORD told Abram, "Leave your country, your relatives, and your father's house, and go to the land that I will show you. I will cause you to become the father of a great nation. I will bless you and make you famous, and I will make you a blessing to others. I will bless those who bless you and curse those who curse you. All the families of the earth will be blessed through you." (Gen. 12:1–3)

The Abrahamic blessing is the central charge of the people of God. It continues in every congregation rooted in a concrete location. Expressed in a variety of ways throughout Scripture, there is a sense that the people of God are to be recipients and then necessarily bearers of blessing to others. A local congregation is called to be a blessing to others, to the neighborhood, and to the world. Missiologist Wilbert Shenk writes,

> The Abrahamic covenant has been called the original Great Commission. . . . It becomes clear that God's strategy for redeeming the world is to call out a people who will be the means by which the nations will learn to know and worship God. This strategy is based on the principle of the "one or the few for the many" (i.e., *pars pro toto*).[23]

The identity of the church emerges out of its essential story. The telling of the story is found primarily in worship. The church is constituted by the Spirit and sustained through the word and sacraments. The word and sacraments are the identity markers for the church. God works powerfully through the word and sacraments, giving life to the church and reminding the church of its identity.

22. Newbigin, *Gospel in Pluralist Society*, 193.

23. Shenk, "New Wineskins." See also Wright, *Mission of God*.

The people of God engage in the worship of God. This sense of worship is to be a lifestyle, but it is also a deliberate activity of the local congregation. "Worship is the strategy by which we interrupt our preoccupation with ourselves and attend to the presence of God. Worship is the time and place that we assign for deliberate attentiveness to God—not because He's confined to time and place but because our self-importance is so insidiously relentless that if we don't deliberately interrupt ourselves regularly, we have no chance of attending to Him at all at other times and in other places."[24] As a pastor, Eugene Peterson began a sermon with three simple, powerful, focusing words: "Let us worship."[25] This worshipping people gathered around the word and sacraments. In the word and at the font, the pool and the table, the church finds its identity. This sense of calling is a constant in the apostolic witness of the New Testament.

For me as a pastor, Sunday worship at Simi Covenant Church was the culmination and high point of my week. It was also the most intense part of my week.[26] The work of ministry throughout the week was shaped by worship. Sunday morning was when our community of faith gathered to sing, to pray, to hear and respond to the word, and to share in the sacraments. I would listen to this assembled people of God worship and be overwhelmed. I would make eye contact with people in the congregation knowing what was happening in their lives, hoping that this time of worship would bring comfort or challenge them. The people gathered in worship is beautiful.

My favorite worship service of the year was Christmas Eve at eleven. The church gathered together to sing carols and hear the Christmas story. It was dark and cold (by California standards). In a candlelit room, the congregation shared in the Lord's Supper just as the clock passed midnight. The service ended, now on Christmas morning, singing, "Joy to the world! The Lord is come!"[27]

The word is preached, and the story is told. Through the preaching and our willingness to hear the word, we become people of witness.[28] This is the narrative of the people of God spoken from the past and made relevant in the contemporary context. This word forms and informs the people of

24. Peterson, *Leap Over a Wall*, 152–53.

25. Collier, "Holy Presence," para. 2.

26. The Evangelical Covenant Church describes worship as reverent, festive, and beautiful (*Covenant Book of Worship*, loc. 272–77 of 11,205.).

27. Watts, "Joy to the World."

28. Hauerwas, *Peaceable Kingdom*, 108.

God. The community gathers around this word and finds life. Christians are people of the book. "Our communal identity is bound up with a set of literary texts that together form canonical Scripture."[29] This scriptural orientation is expressed and lived out through faith traditions within specific cultural contexts.[30] Theologian Stanley Grenz writes,

> Rather than being merely an aggregate of its members, the church is a people imbued with a particular "constitutive narrative," namely the biblical narrative of God bringing creation to is divinely intended goal. The church is a community of the converted, therefore, because the biblical narrative provides its participant with the interpretive framework through which they individually and corporately find their identity as those who are in "Christ" and through which they view life and the world.[31]

The sacraments are celebrated and lived out in the community. These sacraments—baptism and the Lord's Supper, commanded and instituted by Jesus—retell the story of Jesus and form a community image. Theologian Jürgen Moltmann writes, "Just as the Christian church is called into being through the proclamation of the gospel, so through baptism it is called to the freedom of the messianic era. Through baptism it demonstrates the dawn of the rule of God in personal life and in the common conversion to the future of that rule."[32] Grenz and Franke expand on this thought:

> Although the church is constituted by the Spirit, the proclamation of the Word is the vehicle through which the Spirit engages in this constituting work, and such proclamation is ultimately an activity of the church viewed as a community of reference. . . . Baptism and the Lord's Supper are visual sermons in that they recount in a dramatic, symbolic manner the Christian declaration that "God was in Christ reconciling the world to himself" (2 Cor 5:19). . . . Baptism and the Lord's Supper bring not only the narrative past, but also the eschatological future into view. These acts symbolically announce the promise that God will one day bring the divine creative work to completion, but more importantly that this completion constitutes the true identity of the believer, the believing community, and even all creation.[33]

29. Grenz and Franke, *Beyond Foundationalism*, 57.
30. Grenz and Franke, *Beyond Foundationalism*, 93, 130.
31. Grenz, *Renewing the Center*, 323–24.
32. Moltmann, *Church in the Spirit*, 226.
33. Grenz, *Renewing the Center*, 324–25.

Baptism embodies the concept of election to be people of God and forms the basic identity of church from which new forms might emerge. The church is baptized into Christ, into the body of Christ, and into the mission of Christ. Baptism is the rite of initiation. Baptism tells the story of the church's election, and the church becomes part of that story. Baptism marks the individual as part of the community. It is an act of the community. In baptism, people are inducted into a new humanity that transcends all other definitions of identity.

The Lord's Supper is the sustaining meal bringing this identity to mind. It is the feast of the people of God who exist at the margins. The mission of the church is bracketed by the upper-room meal of the Lord and by the eschatological heavenly meal. This space in between is the space of mission sustained by the presence of Christ. All this emerges out of the shared story and history located in the word. The Lord's Supper is the eschatological meal of God's continuing presence to the people of God. Moltmann writes,

> The messianic proclamation of the gospel calls faith into life. The call which believers hear leads them to baptism in Christ's church. This fellowship assembles in worship at the Lord's Table, celebrating its bond with Christ and with one another in the Lord's Supper. Just as baptism is the eschatological sign of starting out, valid once and for all, so the regular and constant fellowship at the table of the Lord is the eschatological sign of being on the way.[34]

The Church as the Body of Christ Is a Community.

There is no such thing as an isolated, individual Christian. The church is a social reality. The church is family, sisters and brothers united in Christ. We are siblings with each other. We are family: not associates, not neighbors, and not even merely friends (certainly not "giving units"!). We are family. The body of Christ welcomes others into the fellowship. The church does life together. It is a place of caring and support. Here the church encourages each other in discipleship. Those in a community love one another in Jesus's name, serve each other, and serve in the neighborhood.

The church is the people of God gathered in Jesus's name as the body of Christ. Paul declares, "You are the body of Christ, and each one of you is a part of it" (1 Cor 12:27). The church as the body of Christ is not merely

34. Moltmann, *Church in the Spirit*, 242–43.

a sociological concept; the church is a mystical communion of members of Christ's body joined together.[35] The church is not merely an assembly of persons; it is a creation of the Spirit.[36] The church is the body of Christ, not just a club; rather, the church is the visible manifestation of Christ. Bonhoeffer writes, "The social significance of the church is decisive—Christ is present only in the church, that is, where the Christian church-community is united by preaching and the Lord's Supper in mutual Christian love."[37]

This becomes reality lived out through the lives of people. The church as the social realty of Christ is a different type of community. The church as an eschatological outpouring of the Spirit sees the elimination of social barriers. The church practices togetherness, or unity, in a bond of love. The church as the body of Christ, as a community, is a group of people who gather together in the name of Jesus. This particular and wonderfully peculiar people worship God, receive the word, celebrate baptism and Eucharist, and care for each other. As people gifted by the Spirit, those in the church serve each other. This people give witness to the good news. They seek to bless the world around them for their neighbors' good. This people spur each other on toward good works. This people bear each other's burdens and nudge each other toward maturity in Christ, Christoformity. This group of people gathers around the word in study and seeks to see how that word applies to their lives. This group of people holds each other accountable. This group rejoices with those who rejoice and weeps with those who weep. This people has open arms toward others. It doesn't built walls but rather longer tables. This is the body of Christ, gathered locally but replicated all over the globe.

I served as pastor in one congregation for twenty-four years. I witnessed the church, this local body of Christ, come together and rally around people in times of celebration and difficulty. As a church we recognized that all of us carried wounds and hurts, but some of us just had better masks. We worked hard to embrace each other, care for each other, forgive each other, and be a safe place for each other, so that the masks could be removed. This happened in formal settings and informally, sometimes just through a chance meeting. Together, the church helped each other to love and do good (Heb 10:24).

35. Dulles, *Models of the Church*, 114.

36. Bevans, "Creation of the Spirit."

37. Bonhoeffer, *Sanctorum Communio*, 138.

The church as the body of Christ exists in the world to engage in the world. This is a new ecclesiology developing out of a sense of the body of Christ existing at the margins in the world. The concept of the body of Christ missionally engaged in the world emerges from an understanding of the incarnation. Following Christ, who stepped into our world, the church must also dwell in the world. From this location, the church is tasked with engaging and blessing the world. As Bonhoeffer forcefully puts it, "The church, like Christ, has become worldly. . . . For the sake of real people, the church must be thoroughly worldly."[38] "The church in mission is, primarily, the local church everywhere in the world."[39]

From this incarnational stance, we understand the servant nature of the church as the earthly-historical body of Christ.[40] The church does not exist in a triumphalist sense; rather, the church exists as servant. The church is the sign, instrument, and foretaste of the kingdom. From this location, the church is able, and actually called, to bless the world in the name of Jesus. Barry Harvey writes, "The doctrine of the incarnation, God made flesh, authorizes the followers of Christ to live unreservedly in the material world without fear of being unfaithful to God."[41] The church is the redeemed humanity that is free to exist for others.[42]

At Simi Covenant, we intentionally engaged our community, as Pietists would say, "for God's glory and our neighbors' good." Not only were we involved in the local homeless care and meal program, but we also hired a person who offered a level of managed care to the people with specific tangible needs who found our church. We opened our facilities to a number of community groups, allowing our space to be used throughout the week.

One of our most significant efforts was helping to plant a Spanish-language congregation that met in our buildings (Nueva Esperanza Covenant Church de Simi Valley). Over time, these long-term guests became a vital second family that used our facilities. At various times in the year, we did ministry projects together in our city and in Mexico and held combined worship services. This was not always easy. Scheduling became more complex. Cultural differences required good listening and compromises. This new congregation was able to minister to segments of our city that the

38. Kelly and Nelson, *Dietrich Bonhoeffer*, 86–87.

39. Bosch, *Transforming Mission*, 378.

40. Harvey, *Can These Bones Live?*, 12.

41. Harvey, *Can These Bones Live?*, 31.

42. Bonhoeffer, *Letters and Papers*, 382.

English language congregation couldn't, and this congregation opened the hearts and minds of Simi Covenant.

The Church Is the Temple of the Spirit.

The church is the temple of the Spirit, empowered by the Spirit to serve, to engage in acts of mercy and justice, and to share the gospel of Jesus so that others might come to know and follow him. The church engages in witness extending itself out beyond the confines of the believers.

While word and sacraments constitute the church in the name of Jesus and create the identity of the church, it is the Spirit who enlivens and empowers the church, making the church a charismatic entity.[43] "It is the presence of God who calls members to himself, sustains them by his grace and works through them as they carry out the mission of the Church."[44] The Spirit calls, equips, and challenges the church to be a missionary church.[45]

The church exists "in the power of the Holy Spirit."[46] The ministries and functions of the church, its gifts and tasks, emerge only from the work of the Spirit of Christ. The post-Easter coming of the Spirit at Pentecost thrusts the people of God into a new day of mission as the body of Christ. In the book of Acts, the church expands at each stage by the initiations of the Holy Spirit, not by human strategies. The church expands as it encounters specific contexts. The gospel responds to the aches, the hurts, the dreams, and the aspirations of a local situation. The local church responds contextually. Pastor-scholar Michael Frost reminds us, "Mission is like water, in that it flows most effectively when hundreds or thousands of nameless, faceless Christians humbly submit to the task of contributing their bucket to the torrent."[47] Wilbert Shenk writes,

> Missionary engagement acknowledges the priority of the context over structure. In the apostolic model of witness the "other" is invited to set the terms of interaction, whether it is an appeal for healing or exorcism or the solution to a perplexing issue. The presence of the witness is essential in making such an exchange possible at all, but whether it actually takes place depends on the

43. Fuellenbach, *Church*, 58, 62.
44. Dulles, *Models of the Church*, 114.
45. Bevans, "Creation of the Spirit," 6.
46. Moltmann, *Church in the Spirit*, 289.
47. M. Frost, *Mission Is Shape of Water*, loc. 237 of 5360.

> attitude and initiative of the other. Giving priority to the context in contemporary culture means two things: (1) an agenda reflecting the heart cries of this culture will emerge; and (2) reading Scripture in light of the angst in contemporary culture will draw us into the Word in new ways.[48]

The Spirit of Christ energizes this new work. The Spirit manifests in the church through the giving of spiritual gifts that are demonstrated through the actions and practices of the church. The Spirit always has priority. Ministries of the Spirit develop at the will of the Spirit. It is the powerful Spirit who is able to engage dry bones and do a new thing that empowers the church. The post-Easter community of Jesus living through a Pentecost experience continues to go forth in mission in the world for the sake of Jesus.

The work of the Spirit of God moves the church beyond institutionalism. The church cannot be static. The Spirit always moves the church into new realms, advancing the gospel. "The church is the work and tool, a sign and a witness of the Spirit of God which fills it."[49] This charismatic nature of the church, gifted by the Spirit of Jesus, is the source and hope for the church.

The faithful are joined together by the Spirit and become the church (1 Pet 2:4–7). "The Church is built up of believers on the foundation stone of Christ—as a spiritual house; not a material earthly temple, nor yet a completely spiritualized temple, but as a pneumatic temple which lives by the *Pneuma* and of which all members are filled and vivified by the *Pneuma*."[50] We are built up into the measure of Christ through the giftings of the Spirit.

The Three Movements of the Local Congregation

These are three movements of the local church as the people of God: *up* in worship (focused on word and sacraments, as the body of Christ), *with* in a community of care and discipleship, and (as the temple of the Spirit) *out* in witness and service to the world. Up, with, out. These three are essential. This is the essential DNA of the local congregation. Every local church needs to be engaged in worship, in discipleship and care, and in witness.

48. Shenk, "Mission, Renewal," 158.
49. Küng, *Church*, 169.
50. Küng, *Church*, 172.

Without all three, the local church is not fully engaged in mission. These dimensions will look different for every congregation, but these three foci are the core emphases of a local congregation. They are foundational. As we will see, the way these are lived out in the life of a local congregation will be a matter of discernment for that body of believers. The call on the church is to discover fresh ways of being the church in the world in the diaspora. The local congregation exists on mission. A congregation does not exist for itself. Reggie McNeal writes,

> The church = the people of God partnering with God in his redemptive mission in the world. This biblical view of church shifts our understanding of it from place and program to a way of being in relationship with God and humanity. It positions followers of Jesus as coconspirators with God in healing the damage caused by sin. Terms such as "people," "partnering," and "in mission" make it clear that the crosshairs of God's purpose are centered on the world, not the church.[51]

A focus on word and community alone creates isolated fellowships that are not living up to their calling beyond the fellowship. A focus on community and the world alone is nothing more than a service club doing good, but without the direction or the empowerment of the Lord. A focus on the word and the world alone illustrates individual believers who serve on their own without the benefit of other believers.

People of God; body of Christ; temple of the Holy Spirit. This is rich theology, but it gets lived out in local contexts. I am committed to the ministry of the local church and its leaders in spite of its flaws, stuttered progress, and messiness. Church has always been a part of my life. I grew up at First Covenant Church in Oakland, California. This church was the center of my family's life and mine. Three generations of my family have been a part of that congregation: my grandparents, my parents, and me. Three generations have served, worshipped, and been nurtured by this church, which is over 125 years old.

At First Covenant Church, Oakland, I was dedicated as an infant and attended Sunday school and youth groups, VBS, and summer camps. I was baptized at First Covenant and first sensed my call to ministry. During my high school years, my pastors allowed me to shadow them as they did their work. Through hours of watching and observing, coaching and mentoring, and hands-on experience, I learned what it meant to be a pastor. In very

51. McNeal, *Kingdom Come*, 136.

ordinary, relational, and intentional ways, my pastors helped form me and gave me a framework for being a pastor.

First Covenant for me was family. It was the place where my faith took root and was nurtured. I was surrounded by surrogate mothers and fathers, aunts and uncles, grandparents, and brothers and sisters. We gathered to worship and to serve, but we did this as family. This made all the difference. People in my church nurtured me and loved me. Older people mentored me. This happened in formal, programmatic ways, as well as informally and relationally. Beyond my parents and brother, I was part of a community of faith with people who loved me along the journey.

After sharing about his home church, Scot McKnight writes, "Everything I learned about the Christian life I learned from my church. I will make this a bigger principle: a local church determines what the Christian life looks like for the people in that church. Now I'll make it even bigger still: we all learn the Christian life from how our local church shapes us. These three principles are a way of saying that local churches matter far more than we often know."[52]

I am who I am today as a person, a pastor, and a professor because of these people: pastors, lay leaders, members of the congregation, and friends. I am grateful for First Covenant Church, my home church. The local church is the focus of mission. In an ordinary church, in relationship with one another, in mundane routines, and in moments of ecstasy, people are discipled and formed.

After graduating from seminary, I joined the pastoral staff at the Evangelical Covenant Church of Simi Valley, California. My wife and I, and then with our two children who came along, were a part of that congregation for forty years. I was on staff at that church for twenty-four years (eighteen of those years as senior pastor). I had the opportunity and the great joy of leading and forming that congregation over decades. Eugene Peterson writes about St. Benedict's vow of stability: "Dwelling in one place over time makes all the difference. A place is what allows stories to develop."[53]

We saw good results. I made a good deal of mistakes along the way. We were a community of faith, worshipping and witnessing. Because of my longevity at that church, I was able to pastor people through many stages of life. I walked with people through the very best and worst of times: births, infant baptisms and dedications, believers' baptisms, birthdays,

52. McKnight, *Fellowship of Differents*, 12.

53. Peterson, "Best Life," para. 48.

graduations, weddings, divorces, illnesses, accidents, and funerals. All the stuff of life.

And my family developed deep, lasting friendships with some in the congregation. We did life together with these people. We raised our kids together. Shared the ups and downs of family life. Cared for each other. Helped each other become better. Held each other in sorrow. Rejoiced in the best of times. In my local congregation, I found a place to grow in my walk with Christ, to serve, to enjoy rich friendships and a good social life, to be cared for in scary moments, and to be comforted in the face of illness and death. All of the wonderful and crazy parts of church move toward one goal: being formed into the image of Christ.

These two congregations, the congregation I grew up in and the congregation I had the privilege of pastoring, have greatly impacted my life. Reflecting on these two congregations, it was the deep social connections between people as sisters and brothers in Christ. The core of both of these congregations was being committed to Christ and to each other. It was evident throughout the life of these congregations. This core commitment shaped me. Over the years, people in these congregations have encouraged me, challenged me, believed in me, and stood by me. I experienced the family of God with all of its benefits.

It was all very ordinary. Human. Earthy. And it was at the same time sacred. In his writing, Wendell Berry reminds us of the very earthiness of our existence. His books like *Jayber Crow* reveal the wonders that happen with people and in community in the mundane routines of life.[54] Eugene Peterson notes,

> Wendell Berry is a writer from whom I have learned much of my pastoral theology. Berry is a farmer in Kentucky. On this farm, besides plowing fields, planting crops, and working horses, he writes novels and poems and essays. The importance of place is a recurrent theme—place embraced and loved, understood and honored. Whenever Berry writes the word "farm," I substitute "parish": the sentence works for me every time.[55]

It is right here, at this very common level, that the congregation is the church and does the work of the gospel. It really isn't very glamorous. Peterson, again, writes that "as a pastor, you've got to be willing to take people as they are. And live with them where they are. And not impose your will

54. See Bartholomew, "5 Reasons"; Childress, "Good Work."

55. Peterson, *Under the Unpredictable Plant*, 131.

on them. Because God has different ways of being with people, and you don't always know what they are."[56] When we get down to the nitty-gritty of it all, it is routine and mundane, day in and day out, with some time on the mountaintop but most of it in the valley.

Church is family. We are on this road together. We laugh, we care, we cry, we worship, we are convicted, we are challenged, we are comforted, we get angry, and we serve. This is church, local, mystery and messy. In the midst of it all, we are being formed into the image of Christ.

This is not Rotary; this is not a local softball league. Those are social gatherings with purpose, and they are wonderful organizations that do good and meet needs. But we are church: in the very local, ordinariness of the church, the Lord meets us. Jesus promised, "Where two or three are gathered, I am there in their midst" (Matt 18:20). When we gather as a congregation, we remember our identity is formed by the word, the font and pool, and the table. As we gather, infused with the power of Jesus Christ by his Spirit, it is a very different gathering. It is here that we are being transformed. It is here that walls of hostility are broken down. It is here that we become one. It is here that we open our arms wide to welcome the marginalized, the sick, the outcast, the sinner.

Congregations are local, made up of real people and sometimes messy. But the congregation is the people of God, body of Christ, temple of the Spirit. Worshipping together, caring for each other, being formed into the image of Christ, empowered by the Spirit to witness, to seek justice, for the good of the neighborhood.

The casseroles, the membership class, the prayer meeting, the workday, as well as worship and weddings and funerals and confirmation are places where the Lord meets us. It is all about being formed. This is the reality of the church. Ordinary. Sometimes it will be very tough, but this is the reality of the messy mystery of church. Nadia Bolz-Weber reminded potential new members to the church:

> I wanted them to hear me: This community will disappoint them. It's a matter of when, not if. We will let them down or I'll say something stupid and hurt their feelings. I then invite them on this side of their inevitable disappointment to decide if they'll stick around after it happens. If they choose to leave when we don't meet their expectations, they won't get to see how the grace of God can come in and fill the holes left by our community's failure, and that's just

56. Peterson, "Faithful to the End," para. 6.

> too beautiful and too real to miss. Welcome to House for All Sinners and Saints. We will disappoint you.[57]

These local expressions of the church are always on mission—sent! Gorman writes, "Paul wanted the communities he addressed not merely to believe the gospel but to become the gospel, and in so doing to participate in the very life and mission of God."[58] Tim Soerens notes, "To become the church in everyday life is not a nice idea for religious people. It's a call for holistic revolution. Our gatherings, our liturgies, and our sermons will remain vital, but not if they are not oriented toward forming us to be the body of Christ in the everyday life of our neighborhoods. We must go on a journey together to recover how to be the church in our actual lives because if we don't, another story will ultimately win the day."[59]

THE CHURCH IN PHILIPPI

Paul dealt with real-life congregations and people. The mystery and the messy. Consider the church in Philippi. Paul had a deep affection for these people. Who were the members of that congregation? There was Lydia, a convert to Judaism who owned her own business and was therefore a woman of means. She gladly received the gospel and was baptized with her entire household (Acts 16:11–15). The church met in her home.

There was a girl who had clairvoyant abilities (Acts 16:16–24). She was influenced by and captive to the powers of the evil one, as well as economic powers. She followed Paul and his team around, becoming quite a nuisance. After some time, Paul spoke to her. And just as Jesus restored people who were captive to evil, this girl was set free from the chains of bondage. By the power of the Spirit of Jesus, the life of this girl changed. And it changed for the girl's captors, who were making money off her condition. The girl's freedom impacted and challenged the prevailing economic systems and injustices of her day.

There was also an unnamed man who worked as a jailer. He had been responsible for guarding Paul and Silas after they had been illegally arrested and flogged for exorcising a spirit from a slave girl. At midnight, God shook the darkened prison to its foundations, waking the sleeping jailer: the cell

57. Bolz-Weber, *Pastrix*, 54–55.

58. Gorman, *Becoming the Gospel*, 2.

59. Soerens, *Everywhere You Look*, 14.

doors flew open and the chains binding all the prisoners came loose. Thinking the prisoners had escaped, the jailer moved to kill himself. But Paul intervened, assuring him that no one had left. Confronted simultaneously by the frightening power of God and the mercy that spared his life, the man fell to his knees and believed. And as with Lydia, his whole household was baptized (Acts 16:16–34).

Later, in prison again, Paul wrote to his friends in Philippi, remembering fondly their partnership with him and each other in the cause of the gospel. He encouraged them to continue their unity in the Spirit, "being confident of this, that he who began a good work in you will carry it on to completion until the day of Christ Jesus" (Phil 1:6). We can imagine that as he wrote those words, he was thinking of Lydia, the girl who had been enslaved, the jailer, and others who were as different as they could be, yet still one in Christ. He was also thinking about Euodia and Syntyche, who apparently had a conflict to work out (Phil 4:2–3). Neither social nor interpersonal differences dampened Paul's conviction that God was at work in this congregation, in and among ordinary people in a concrete place. And then Paul writes in Phil 1,

> So it is right that I should feel as I do about all of you, for you have a special place in my heart. You share with me the special favor of God, both in my imprisonment and in defending and confirming the truth of the Good News. God knows how much I love you and long for you with the tender compassion of Christ Jesus. (Phil 1:7–8 NLT)

It was just an ordinary church, but it was living out the gospel in mission. This church embodied Gal 3:28: "There is neither Jew nor Gentile, neither slave nor free, nor is there male and female, for you are all one in Christ Jesus." This church broke through barriers: ethnic, economic, gender. This is the call on all congregations in context.[60] But every congregation must determine how to break through barriers and break down walls in order to build longer tables. Every local congregation is called to mission in a particular place. In that place the church worships, cares and disciples, and witnesses. It will be different for each congregation, but the church

60. The church growth movement distorted the gospel with an application of the homogeneous unit principle. It is an accurate observation that people do not want to cross lines to hear the gospel, but this must not become the prescription for growing congregations. The local congregation is to embody the gospel, breaking through these barriers. This is tough. It will cause disruption and chaos. It will be uncomfortable, but this is gospel. See Tizon, *Christ Among the Classes*.

must not be settled and content. It is rooted and sent, with eyes that look beyond the immediate walls.

Dietrich Bonhoeffer, in a different time and out of his own sense of frustration over the irrelevance of the church institution, wrote prophetically, offering a picture of a church reimagined:

> The church is only the church when it exists for others. To make a start, it should give away all its property to those in need. The clergy must live solely on the free-will offerings of their congregations, or possibly engage in some secular calling. The church must share in the secular problems of ordinary human life, not dominating, but helping and serving. It must tell men of every calling what it means to live in Christ, to exist for others.[61]

Pope Francis said it this way: "I prefer a Church which is bruised, hurting, and dirty because it has been out on the streets, rather than a Church which is unhealthy from being confined and from clinging to its own security."[62] The root paradigm of the church had to shift from a "come and see" mentality where we built attracting buildings and programs, to a "go and dwell," apostolic, culture-infiltrating stance.[63]

This is the call on every congregation—to be salt and light in our world. In spite of the ordinariness and even difficulties of a particular congregation, every church, like the church in Philippi, will shine like stars in the sky, holding firmly to the word of life (Phil 2:15). Missiologist David Bosch describes evangelism (but I think this also speaks to the wider work of the church):

> That dimension of activity of the church's mission which seeks to offer every person, everywhere, a valid opportunity to be directly challenged by the gospel of explicit faith in Jesus Christ, with a view to embracing him as Savior, becoming a living member of his community, and being enlisted in his service of reconciliation, peace and justice on earth.[64]

This is the work, the mission of every congregation and every follower of Jesus. This is done in unique ways for each believer and every congregation,

61. Bonhoeffer, *Letters and Papers*, 282.

62. Francis, *Joy of the Gospel*, 28.

63. Gibbs and Bolger, *Emerging Churches*, 236.

64. Quoted in Sunquist and Yong, *Gospel and Pluralism Today*, 175.

but the press of the gospel, the compelling love of Jesus, urges us in this task.

Missionary and scholar Alan Kreider notes that the early church grew not because of programs, dazzling worship, or celebrity pastors but rather because of a "patient ferment." Followers of Jesus simply lived out their lives in Jesus's name. This was a sweet aroma (2 Cor 2) that led people into the fellowship. Because of an ethic of love—love for fellow believers, the neighbor, the other, strangers, and the marginalized—the mission of Christ advanced. Kreider writes,

> The ferment was spontaneous, and it involved ordinary ingredients that at times synergized into a heady brew. The churches grew in many places, taking varied forms. They proliferated because the faith that these fishers and hunters embodied was attractive to people who were dissatisfied with their old cultural and religious habits, who felt pushed to explore new possibilities, and who then encountered Christians who embodied a new manner of life that pulled them toward what the Christians called "rebirth" into a new life. Surprisingly, this happened in a patient manner.[65]

Followers of Jesus were simply attractive to the world around them. Jesus said, "A new command I give you: Love one another. As I have loved you, so you must love one another. By this everyone will know that you are my disciples, if you love one another" (John 13:34–35).

This is the power of the Spirit at work in followers of Jesus and in a local congregation. Christianity grew at an amazing rate, perhaps 40 percent a decade, within the Roman Empire, primarily due to the witness and informal proclamation of the gospel by "ordinary" Christians.[66]

The Letter to Diognetus, likely written sometime between the early second century and the late second century (around AD 150–200), gives us a glimpse of what was happening in the earliest days of the church:

> Christians are not differentiated from other people by country, language or customs; you see, they do not live in cities of their own, or speak some strange dialect or have some peculiar lifestyle. They live in both Greek and foreign cities, wherever chance has put them. They follow local customs in clothing, food, and the other aspects of life. But at the same time, they demonstrate to us the wonderful and certainly unusual form of their own citizenship. They live

65. Kreider, *Patient Ferment of Church*, 12.

66. Bevans and Schroeder, *Prophetic Dialogue*, loc. 1961–63 of 3767.

> in their own native lands, but as aliens; as citizens, they share all things with others; but like aliens suffer all things. Every foreign country is to them as their native country, but every native land is a foreign country. They are treated outrageously and behave respectfully to others. When they do good, they are punished as evil doers; when punished, they rejoice as if being given new life. They are attacked by Jews as aliens, and are persecuted by Greeks; yet those who hate them cannot give any reason for their hostility. To put it simply—the soul is to the body as Christians are to the world. The soul is spread through all parts of the body and Christians through all the cities of the world. The soul is in the body but is not of the body; Christians are in the world but not of the world.[67]

THE CONCRETE LOCAL CHURCH

This gospel work occurs in very local contexts, missional outposts. A local congregation needs to extend itself beyond the walls of a church.[68] This will require looking at the context of every congregation in new ways and celebrating the ordinariness of a church in its context. Since every congregation is rooted in a particular place, a congregation needs to understand that place where it is rooted. A congregation needs to see, really see, where it is located.

Every congregation must take a walk![69] A congregation walks its neighborhood, slowly, praying with open eyes and ears and noses and quietly reflecting and observing. What do we see, what do we hear, and what do we smell? Where is the joy? Where is the heartache?

After a congregation takes the walk, it is then able to ask the questions: Who are we called to be in this place, this neighborhood? Why do we exist? What are the needs? What are the aches and hurts? What are the hopes? Who are my neighbors? What gospel hope are we as a congregation able to offer? How might we serve and bless? What tangible, messy ways can we be Christ's people here? A congregation must engage in a practice of discernment.[70]

67. Translation based on Meecham, *Epistle to Diognetus*, 151–52.

68. See Pathak and Runyon, *Art of Neighboring*.

69. Roxburgh, *Joining God, Remaking Church*, 102.

70. See Roxburgh, *Joining God, Remaking Church*, 102; Hayden, *Remissioning Church*, 58–61. See also Edwards, "Lectio Vicinitas."

The Local Church in Three Locations

David Fitch suggests each congregation should be present in three locations (identified with the language of a circle): the close circle, the dotted circle, and the half circle.[71] Each of these is important in the missional life of a church. Each person in a congregation can determine how to situate themselves in each of these circles.

Rather than a new program, this framework helps a congregation begin to see itself as a missional outpost. Every follower of Jesus can begin to see the spaces that they occupy in normal life, as a place where they can "shine like stars" (Phil 2:13). In all of these locations, the church is on mission forming disciples, engaging in worship and care, and being a witness in sending. Fitch writes,

> All three circles are part and parcel of each discipline on the move. This is a pattern throughout the New Testament. The church gathers in its place of worship to encounter Christ's presence. But this same church is sent out to extend his presence into our homes, our neighborhoods, and among the marginalized and hurting in the world. The church's location therefore cannot be seen in terms of in here or out there. It is an entire way of life.[72]

The first circle is the close circle. This is where followers of Jesus assemble. This is the church gathered for worship around the word and the font and the table. The second circle is the dotted circle. This is where followers of Jesus and others gather in the neighborhood. This is the church beyond the walls of the church. This is the church caring for others in the congregation. This is the people of God engaged with neighbors, caring for others, opening up homes in acts of hospitality, and creating opportunities for prayer and study. This is the church doing acts of service. The third circle is the half circle. Here followers of Jesus enter into the neighborhood, the world, as guests. This is the people of God engaged in the world. Here, followers of Christ live out their call to love others. This is done through a sense of humility and sacrifice. Here the gospel might be shared with others.

71. Fitch, *Seven Practices for Church*, 11.

72. Fitch, *Faithful Presence*, 41.

First Peter 3:15–17 can be a key guide for how followers of Jesus engage in the world as a witness:

> Instead, you must worship Christ as Lord of your life. And if someone asks about your hope as a believer, always be ready to explain it. But do this in a gentle and respectful way. Keep your conscience clear. Then if people speak against you, they will be ashamed when they see what a good life you live because you belong to Christ. Remember, it is better to suffer for doing good, if that is what God wants, than to suffer for doing wrong!

Followers of Jesus witness to others in their neighborhood according to these words: "First of all, believers commit to follow Jesus in the way they live their daily lives. Then as others see the compelling love of Jesus in their lives, those people ask about it. This gives followers the opportunity to "gossip the gospel."[73] This is done gently and respectfully.

The church cannot be cloistered where it is safe. The church engages in a faithful presence. Again, this isn't a program. This is simply people living their lives as devoted followers of Jesus, seeking to be more like him, and loving God, each other in the church, and their neighbor in the world. This is the church living out its mission.

The church is always local, and each congregation is unique. Real people. Ordinary people. Striving to follow Christ. Something wonderful can happen here. It has its own story based on location, size, history of successes and challenges, pastors, worship style, and facilities.[74] Every congregation can celebrate its unique story. All congregations sent, not settled, can celebrate how they are impacting their world as they worship, disciple, and care.

73. Green, *Evangelism in Early Church*, 173.

74. See Galindo, *Hidden Lives of Congregations*.

3

Who

Followers of Jesus are a community of priests. By virtue of our baptism, all who follow Jesus are called into mission. This calling is on every believer. The apostle Peter writes,

> But you are a chosen people, a royal priesthood, a holy nation, God's special possession, that you may declare the praises of him who called you out of darkness into his wonderful light. Once you were not a people, but now you are the people of God; once you had not received mercy, but now you have received mercy. (1 Pet 2:9–10)

One of the greatest hindrances to the gospel task within congregations is the development of the clergy class. Over time, the gifting of a pastor became more institutionalized. "Pastor" became a title, a certification, and a job. Pastors became experts. They had the proper skills and techniques to do work in the church structure. This led to the development of the professionalization of pastors, a separate and hierarchal class in the church known as clergy.

This clergy/laity divide has hamstrung the body of Christ. The fullness of the gifts of Christ's followers are overlooked and underutilized. It has kept people in local congregations from recognizing their gifts and talents and using them the Christ's work. The church has been hindered. Followers of Jesus are deprived of the joy of using their lives, gifts, and talents to serve others, to give themselves away.

A call to ministry on anyone's life is a call to service, not to privilege. This is particularly true for those called clergy. In too many cases, an emphasis on the clergy class has led to inflated egos and ministerial malpractice. This clergy class distinction, which elevates certain persons to levels of prestige and power, has led to significant hurt and abuse in the body of Christ. This can be characterized by ego, pride, and lust. Similar to what occurs in politics and in the business world, this is a serious blight on the church.[1]

"I'm just a layperson" is a phrase that should never be used in the church. All persons in a congregation who are followers of Jesus, women and men, are called and gifted to serve. The apostle Paul writes,

> There are different kinds of gifts, but the same Spirit distributes them. There are different kinds of service, but the same Lord. There are different kinds of working, but in all of them and in everyone it is the same God at work. Now to each one the manifestation of the Spirit is given for the common good. (1 Cor 12:4–7)

No one person, pastor or otherwise, has all the giftings necessary for a congregation to minister well in a faith community or in the neighborhood. A congregation is richer, a congregation is stronger, and a congregation is mobilized as people in a local setting discover, test out, and strengthen their gifts for service within the congregation and beyond. Without this mobilization, a congregation is prone to simply be a settled group.

Paul gives us examples of what those gifts might be. These are not exclusive lists, but rather examples of the ways that the Spirit of God gifts the church so that it might more effectively do the work of Christ.

> To one there is given through the Spirit a message of wisdom, to another a message of knowledge by means of the same Spirit, to another faith by the same Spirit, to another gifts of healing by that one Spirit, to another miraculous powers, to another prophecy, to another distinguishing between spirits, to another speaking in different kinds of tongues, and to still another the interpretation of tongues. All these are the work of one and the same Spirit, and he distributes them to each one, just as he determines.
>
> Just as a body, though one, has many parts, but all its many parts form one body, so it is with Christ. For we were all baptized by one Spirit so as to form one body—whether Jews or Gentiles, slave or free—and we were all given the one Spirit to drink. Even so the body is not made up of one part but of many. (1 Cor 12:8–14)

1. See books on clergy abuse: DeGroat, *When Narcissism Comes*; McKnight and Barringer, *Church Called Tov*; Langberg, *Redeeming Power*.

Every follower of Jesus is able to make a difference in their church and their world. When people serve within the church teaching; serving; participating in workdays, music, arts, and more, the church is enriched. In homes, through hospitality and care, Bible study, meals, and encouragement, the church lives out the work of Christ. In the broader world, followers of Jesus extend the goodness and justice of God. These are places where Christ followers are able to engage with others. Here they can be salt and light. Here they can shine as a bright light in a difficult world.

> Christ has no body but yours,
> No hands, no feet on earth but yours,
> Yours are the eyes with which he looks
> Compassion on this world,
> Yours are the feet with which he walks to do good,
> Yours are the hands, with which he blesses all the world.
> Yours are the hands, yours are the feet,
> Yours are the eyes, you are his body.
> Christ has no body now but yours,
> No hands, no feet on earth but yours,
> Yours are the eyes with which he looks
> compassion on this world.
> Christ has no body now on earth but yours.[2]

Followers of Jesus in local congregations serve and benefit the world around them, their neighborhood. In very ordinary and routine, even mundane, ways, followers of Jesus are salt and light. They are a sweet aroma. They shine like stars. This is not simply the work of clergy or those called to leadership roles. This is the task, the responsibility, and the opportunity for all followers of Jesus to do good toward others in the church and in the world. Ordinary Christians, because of their location in their context and neighborhoods, can have an incredible impact on those around them.

But the church has gotten stuck. The church has often become a rigid institution that relies heavily on a clergy class. The rise of centralized organizations with a sense of bureaucracy is a result of modernity and rationality. Guder writes,

> Neither the structures nor the theology of our established Western traditional churches is missional. They are shaped by the legacy of Christendom. That is, they have been formed by centuries in which Western civilization considered itself formally and officially

2. Teresa of Ávila, "Christ Has No Body."

> Christian. . . . Even when the legal structures of Christendom have been removed (as in North America), the legacy continues as a pattern of powerful traditions, attitudes, and social structures.[3]

The church capitulates to the dominant strains of culture. Richard Halverson writes,

> The church moved to Greece, where it became a philosophy. Then it moved to Rome, where it became an institution. Next, it moved to Europe, where it became a culture. And, finally, it moved to America, where it became an enterprise.[4]

Congregations must reclaim the priesthood of all believers. All are called to use their gifts for the benefit of others. This will be disruptive, especially for clergy who enjoy a privileged status and whose ego needs are met through a sense of being needed, who relish the acclaim of others. It is a radical shift. Disruptive, but needed. The pastoral role, while still essential, will have to change. That change begins in the humble and kind heart and will of pastoral leaders. The pastoral leaders of these congregations become missionary pastors. The work done by these pastors is done in a "missionary key."[5]

When the church played a dominant role in society, it was easier to depend upon the clergy to "run the church," to be about the tasks of preaching and teaching, baptizing and gathering people at the Lord's Table, officiating at weddings and funerals, and visiting people in their homes or the hospital. But the world has changed. Again, we need to embrace this reality: "The day of the professional minister is over. The day of the missionary pastor has come. . . . The day of the churched culture is over. The day of the mission field has come."[6] The church in North America must change in order to minister faithfully and missionally.

Whether we like it or not, the ways church has been done, as good as they were, is not the way church will be in the future. The Lord is inviting the church, including every local manifestation of the church, to act in new ways. We must reimagine the role of ministry leaders. Ministry leaders do play an important role, but they are not to be the only ones who do ministry.

3. Guder, "Missional Vocation," 6.
4. As quoted in Woodruff, "Forgotten Letter 'D,'" para. 1.
5. Francis, *Joy of the Gospel*, 21.
6. Callahan, *Effective Church Leadership*, 3, 13.

Their task is to equip the church to engage in the work of ministry. Pastor and missional scholar Alan Roxburgh writes,

> Luke-Acts and Ephesians demonstrate that the Spirit continually pushes the church, in its particular time and place, to reenter the story of Jesus Christ in order to wrestle with the question of how this narrative is given structure in terms of institutions and organizations. As the social and cultural contexts continue to change, the Spirit continually invites and empowers the church to discern the ways that its institutions and structures must be reshaped, reformed.[7]

APOSTLES, PROPHETS, EVANGELISTS, PASTORS, AND TEACHERS

All Christ followers are called and gifted for ministry; the apostle Paul talks about some specific ministries in the church for which people are set apart. This "setting apart" does not necessarily equate with a formal office or ordination. Rather, this setting apart is a recognition of giftings the Lord gives to some followers of Jesus for the purpose of equipping God's people for the work of ministry. These persons may be ordained or not. They may serve full-time in a congregation or ministry, or part-time in a co-vocational role. These set-apart persons are simply called and gifted for certain roles in the church. The apostle Paul writes,

> Now these are the gifts Christ gave to the church: the apostles, the prophets, the evangelists, and the pastors and teachers. Their responsibility is to equip God's people to do his work and build up the church, the body of Christ. (Eph 4:11–12)

Apostles, prophets, evangelists, pastors, and teachers are called to equip God's people to do that work of ministry. All of these giftings continue to function in the church.

Apostles are those who advance the gospel geographically and socially, into new areas and new people groups. They are visionaries who foster a sense of urgent mission and create new movements that spread the gospel. Prophets are those who stand up and stand against social orders that are in opposition to ways of Jesus. They shine the light of the gospel on injustice. They advocate and care for the poor and the oppressed. They hold

7. Roxburgh, *Structured for Mission*, loc. 870–73 of 2947.

the church accountable to engage with "the least of these."[8] Evangelists are those share the gospel with others and invite them to experience the good news of Jesus Christ. They welcome people into God's family. Shepherds (pastors) are those who nurture a congregation as family in worship, discipleship, care, and witness. They seek to bring healing and wholeness to a church. They guide and guard those entrusted to their care. Teachers are those who foster a learning environment, encouraging others to faithfully dwell in Scripture and to hear God's story, provoking the mind, encouraging the heart, and leading toward discipleship. They help to make Scripture accessible and relevant to specific contexts.[9]

All are gifted and all are called to serve in different capacities and in different ways. It is not the apostles, prophets, evangelists, pastors, and teachers who do all the work of ministry, but rather build up and equip the church extending the mission of Christ. Elton Trueblood points out, "The ministry is for all who are called to share in Christ's life, the pastorate is for those who possess the peculiar gift of being able to help other men and women to practice any ministry to which they are called."[10]

"Equipping the saints for ministry" can sound exhausting for ministry leaders. Finding, training, mentoring, and encouraging others to serve takes a great deal of time and work. New structures are required. Ministry leaders will need to shift their priorities and allocate their time and energy in different ways. "Equipping" cannot simply be another task to add to everything else that is being done. There is no doubt that it is often easier just to do the work yourself, but the impact can be exponential when others serve as well.

Of course, we have to admit that some pastors don't want others to serve. Some pastors need to be needed. They need to be the ones who show up, get the work done, and receive the thanks and the accolades. This too must be resisted and overcome.

The conversations about these five giftings gets a bit muddled as it is applied in local settings and personally. Some people hold the title of

8. Richard Rohr writes, "The prophet is not an outsider throwing rocks, nor a comfortable insider who defends the status quo; but one who lives precariously with two perspectives held tightly together in a loving and creative tension: the faithful insider and the critical outsider" (Center for Action and Contemplation, "Edge of the Inside," para. 5).

9. See Woodward, *Creating a Missional Culture*, 45–54 (ch. 3), 121–22; Hayden, *Remissioning Church*, 71.

10. Trueblood, *Incendiary Fellowship*, 41.

apostle, prophet, evangelist, pastor, or teacher. Others don't have such a title but serve in ways that can be characterized as apostolic, prophetic, evangelistic, pastoral, or teaching. This gets lived out in different ways. The confusion arises with the difference between organic leadership and more structured leadership. We see this even in the New Testament. The Pauline Letters have a more organic sense of ministry roles. The Pastoral Letters begin to develop a more formalized approach to church leadership.

And, of course, no one can be, or should be, boxed into certain categories. People who have the title and/or role of pastor can also have giftings in other areas (evangelistically, prophetically, etc.). Every follower of Jesus is a unique blend of giftings and temperaments, influenced greatly by family background, experiences, social location, and more. The Lord uses each person in particular ways to serve in the church and beyond.

When these giftings function within a local congregation, and when clergy allow and encourage these giftings in a local congregation, a new mood of fellowship and ministry emerges within a local body. In local settings, pastors—those who are called to serve in a congregation—are too often the gatekeepers or the permission givers. Pastors within a system can be a bottleneck who restrict ministry, or they can be the ones who encourage ministry. Pastors can clamp down on potential ministry because they will lose control or a sense of admiration by parishioners, or because some mistakes might be made along the way. Or, pastors and ministry leaders can create an atmosphere of innovation, experimentation, and allow for some mistakes and failures. Pastors may get threatened. It is a different style of ministry and emphasis, but it is key to the life of the church in that context.

These Giftings Within a Local Congregation

Chapter 1 referenced the concept from Ralph Winter (missiologist and founder of the US Center for World Mission) of two types of God's redemptive mission in the world. I advocate for the local church as a place of mission that involves aspects of institution and movement. The local church exists as a modality and a sodality as these fivefold gifts are in action. Working together, the church is able to thrive and live into its missional calling.

Both outward-facing apostles, prophets, and evangelists and congregation-focused pastors and teachers are necessary! Apostles, prophets, and evangelists continue to push the church forward with an emphasis in witness and sending. Pastors and teachers minister to the congregation in worship and care and discipleship. One represents the stable institution, the other an advancing movement. The local church that embodies the mission of the church must have internal and external dimensions. The local congregation must embrace both modes of ministry.

An apostolic imagination, pastoring in a missionary key, yearns to see where God is acting in the world and invites the people of God to join them in those places. Apostles keep to an inherited faith and also are committed to the edges, exploring new ideas and territories. This apostolic imagination commits leaders to being storytellers, prophets, and missionaries. This is the ongoing missional impulse of every congregation. It is encouraged by the pastors of that local church. Gorman writes,

> [This is] a mindset that issues inevitably in loving, cruciform inward-focused (i.e., community-focused, or centripetal) and outward-focused (i.e., centrifugal) praxis . . . the normal distinction between "pastoral" and "missional" action (and between "pastoral" and "evangelistic") collapses, since the ultimate good of the other is the focus of all action: entrance into or growth in the reality of God's project to save humanity.[11]

This diagram illustrates how the five ministry functions found in Eph 4 interact with each other and how the local congregation operates as both movement and institution, incorporating both modality and sodality.

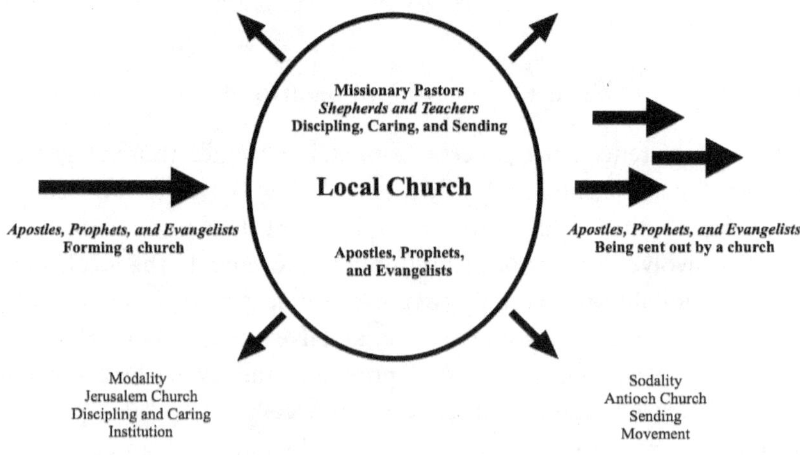

11. Gorman, *Becoming the Gospel*, 39.

The diagram highlights the central focus of the local church. This church is overseen by missionary pastors who are gifted as pastors and teachers. They serve the local faith community in areas of worship, witness, discipleship, and care. These leaders may be ordained clergy, but they share the responsibility of the congregation with other gifted leaders who may or may not be theologically trained and may be in a staff role or lay leaders. There are others in the congregation who have pastoral and teaching gifts. These are to use those gifts alongside congregational leaders for caring and teaching ministries. Those who have responsibility of the congregation as leaders are called to encourage and equip others who are gifted to live out their ministry vocation.

While the functions of a pastor and teacher are vital in the local congregation, these are not the only tasks assumed by church leaders in the local community of faith. The roles of apostle, prophet, and evangelist must be part of the gift mix of the local congregation. Within the congregation are also those who have apostolic, prophetic, and evangelistic gifts. Those with these gifts use their giftings to serve the congregation and the local community in areas of extending mission, justice, evangelism, outreach, and church planting. The pastors who have responsibility for the congregation are again called to encourage and equip others who are gifted to live out their ministry passions. This will stretch some pastors. This will be uncomfortable. This will require giving ministry away, releasing control, and moving beyond the command-and-control approach pastors often take.

It is essential that the pastors/teachers in a congregation affirm and support the work of apostles, prophets, and evangelists. Those with the giftings of apostle, prophet, and evangelist may be the ones who birthed a congregation or new ministry in the first place. They were on the risky front line of ministry. They move into new, unknown, unexplored, and risky territory. They serve off the map.[12] Those with these gifts are a restless bunch and usually don't have the temperament or giftedness for local ministry over the long haul. Local churches are the result of apostles, prophets, and evangelists who moved into a new area to plant this congregation. As the apostle Paul did in the days of the early church, a church was planted and then leadership was given over to others with shepherding and caring gifts.

Some who have apostolic, prophetic, and evangelistic gifts will use those within a congregation to serve the church and the neighborhood. Others with these gifts will be sent out by the congregation to plant new

12. See Gibbs, *Rebirth of the Church*.

congregations in other areas. Thus, the ministry of this local congregation is multiplied.

Those who oversee local congregations as pastors and teachers have a responsibility to the congregation but also to ministry beyond the confines of the church. While ministry leaders, by giftedness and temperament, may tend to focus on pastoral or teaching work, they are responsible, regardless of their primary giftings, to see that the church embraces its full mission.

The driving motif through all this is a sense of pastoring in a missionary key. Pastors cannot sit back in their office. They must be engaged in the street. The job description of the modern pastor will radically change from professional technician, therapist, or manager to that of missionary, spending significant time with local culture.[13] Recall this previous quote: "The day of the professional minister is over. The day of the missionary pastor has come. . . . The day of the churched culture is over. The day of the mission field has come."[14] This is a significant shift for pastoral ministry. It is a catalytic change.

Those who serve as pastors within a congregation are the missional equippers who encourage the outward-facing missional giftings of apostle, prophet, and evangelist while also encourage the teaching, caring, and discipling functions of the congregation as pastors and teachers. Pastors will not be the sole missionaries in a congregation. Some pastors won't have a "missionary gift mix." But local church pastors serving in that missionary key will be the catalysts and the encouragers for ongoing missional engagement. For pastors to serve in this capacity, they will have to let go of control and power! "Pastoral identity must change: the pastor must not stare primarily into the sanctuary, but she or he must also focus on and animate the same horizon the congregation has in view—outward toward the world."[15] Theologian James Fowler puts it this way:

> Pastoral care consists of all the ways a community of faith, under pastoral leadership, intentionally sponsors the awakening, shaping, rectifying, healing, and ongoing growth in vocation of Christian persons and community, under the pressure and power of the in-breaking kingdom of God.[16]

13. Roxburgh, "Missional Leadership," 196–98.
14. Callahan, *Effective Church Leadership*, 3, 13.
15. Small, "Missional Ordered Ministry," 230.
16 Fowler, *Faith Development*, loc. 140–41 of 1515.

The giftings of apostles, prophets, evangelists, pastors, and teachers within a congregation encourage people to be formed increasingly into the image of Christ. This is the work of the church. I think about this work this way:

The goal of pastoral ministry in a local setting is:

> Forming people/a congregation into the image of Christ (discipleship) in the context of the local church (community) on mission (*missio Dei*).

The fivefold leadership gifting is necessary for the church to live into this mission. As these giftings emerge, the local church becomes an ecology of care, transformation, and mission that moves a congregation from sickness to healing, immaturity to maturity, and being settled to being sent. This is the shape of a local congregation on mission in worship, discipleship, care, and witness.

MY MINISTRY SHIFT

I believe in the church, but that has not always been easy. I was sitting in a hotel room in Chicago with a friend and pastoral colleague a decade into being senior pastor. I said, "I am going to go back home, quit my job at church, and get a real job!" He said, "You can do that. I will support you in that. But you won't be happy." When I asked why, he responded, "Because you are called." And I told him, "But I don't want to be called!"

This was a crisis time for me. I was face-to-face with the joy and the burden of serving in a local congregation as pastor. My conversation with my friend Ron was the culmination of a very difficult period of ministry. I had been working very hard, pushing in new directions, and receiving support and encouragement, while also receiving a fair share of criticism, including a questioning of motives. We had bought some more property and built a new worship center. People were looking at our church and were quite impressed. And I was rather impressed too!

But something was unsettling for me. There was a sense of hollowness in my ministry. Maybe I was too caught up in the success of the church and my own success as well. I felt like I was playing to a fickle crowd. I felt that I was responsible for this ministry: "If I don't do it, who will?" When things went well, while I spiritually and piously gave credit to God, it seemed like my doing; when the church did not thrive as it should, it seemed like my fault.

From my years as a teenager, I knew that church work was my passion and my calling. Paul's words in 2 Cor 5:17 have been a touchstone verse in my life: "Therefore, if anyone is in Christ, he is a new creation; the old has gone, the new has come!" That verse with the promise of God transforming people and communities drove my life. This verse expressed my deep passion. I was not ashamed of the gospel.

Yet I was getting away from that conviction. So caught up in the mechanics of the church, my ministry was going stale. My effectiveness seemed meager. My church (and with too much bravado I did call it *my* church then) was attracting crowds, but too often it was church people coming from other locations; soon they would be moving on. I sensed that my church was shuffling churchgoers from one church to the next. For all of our activity (and we had lots of activity), we were making very little impact beyond our nice, safe Christian world.[17] I was discouraged. I was at a breaking point. Since that time, I have discovered that I was not alone in this feeling. Church leaders long for opportunities to be engaged in ministry that transforms. They second-guess their call. Morale is low. Church leaders like me grieve and ache.

So, I decided to quit. The only way, I thought, to be effective as a follower of Jesus was out in the world. I felt that the best thing I could do was resign as pastor, get a "real job" in the secular marketplace, and be the best Christian there—influencing for good in Jesus's name. I interviewed with a friend of mine who was a partner at a marketing company, but I realized very quickly that I was not destined for this new line of work.

There was something tugging at my heart. Theologically, it was a sense of pastoral call upon my life: a wonderful, joyful burden. The apostle Paul speaks about his burden for the church (Gal 4:19; 2 Cor 11:28). I understood that weight. I sensed the weight of God's call to ecclesial ministry on my life. I was to be part of the church, working in and through the church.

So, I reengaged in the life of the church. I believed in the church (and still do!). I began to look at North America as a mission frontier and the

17. This is a bit cynical, but Chuck Swindoll recounts a significant event from the 1800s: "When the Great Exhibition of the Works of Industry of All Nations was opened by Queen Victoria in 1851, people flocked to Hyde Park to behold what they called the 'marvels.' The magic power back then was steam . . . steam plows, [the] steam organ, a steam cannon. The prize went to a steam-driven invention that had 7000 parts—all kinds of pulleys, bells, whistles, and gears . . . gears that meshed with other gears that hummed in harmony and whirled in perfect synchronization. It was a sight to behold. Interestingly, it accomplished nothing" (*Rise and Shine*, 50). Sometimes this feels like what happens at a highly programmed church.

church as a mission outpost on that frontier. This basic shift caused me to pastor differently. I helped the congregation I served to see that we were living on a mission field; church, as we knew it, would have to change. And I had to change. I determined that I would not do church the old way. The root paradigm of the church had to shift from a "come and see" mentality where we built attractive buildings and programs, to a "go and dwell," apostolic, culture-infiltrating stance[18] with an apostolic imagination[19] that would permeate the pastoral vocation and be evident in daily tasks of pastoral leaders.

This shift will look different for each ministry leader. The key is to be open so that the Lord might work in new ways. This will cause adjustment. This change begins at our core. It is an issue of missional Christoformity for the pastor. It is a servant attitude, humility, and letting go.

A shift in a church's focus is not easy. For me, this transition was very painful at times, but it was a transition for the good. The focus of the church changed, but more than that, a change occurred inside of me. For too long, I had a ministry that focused on what I could do and accomplish. This wasn't intentional, but on reflection it was true. I had a rather triumphal and arrogant sense of ministry. The process of reevaluating church shook me to the core. A new stance in life was emerging from deep within, a stance of weakness and humility rather than triumph.

PASTORS[20]

I believe in the church and, even more than before, I have great hope for the church—this messy and full-of-mystery church. The local congregation that gathers for worship, discipleship, fellowship, witness, and service has the ability to impact lives and the world. Only the local church that can do this. Lesslie Newbigin reminds us that the local congregation is the hermeneutic of the gospel; the local congregation makes the gospel credible.[21] The local church is made up of normal, ordinary people who dream big dreams, people who sometimes get caught up in conflicts, people who sincerely desire to love God and others; but people—gathered in a local

18. Gibbs and Bolger, *Emerging Churches*, 236.

19. Hirsch, *Forgotten Ways*, 125, 292; Hirsch and Catchim, *Permanent Revolution*.

20. An earlier form of this material appeared in Lee and Fredrickson, *That Their Work*.

21. Newbigin, *Gospel in Pluralist Society*, 227.

congregation—make the gospel credible for the world and serve the world! Who is able for this task? Not us on our own, but only in the power of God. Paul reminds us, "But we have this treasure in jars of clay to show that this all-surpassing power is from God and not from us" (2 Cor 4:7).

Pastors play an essential role in the work of a local congregation. They are not the only ministers, but they serve in a special way. Women and men are called into ministry and exhibit gifts, attributes, and passions that suit them for ministry. All who follow Jesus are priests, and the task of ministry belongs to the whole church. Yet we must not minimize the marvelous call to pastoral ministry on women and men. As Pastor Richard John Neuhaus has written, "Those who have been touched by the burning coal from the altar, and whose touch has been ratified by the call of the Church, must not pretend that nothing special has happened to them."[22]

The call to pastoral ministry comes from God. It is not a static thing that can be possessed. To say that one "has" a call is not quite right. Better to say that one "is called" to emphasize that it is a continual summons into a particular relationship of faithfulness to the one who calls. Ministry begins as a gifting by God and from God. It is God who calls people; it is God who gifts people. True ministry is not a mere human doing, but is empowered by the Holy Spirit (1 Thess 1:4–5). Bishop and professor Will Willimon reminds us, "Ministry is therefore something that God does through the church before it is anything we do. Our significance, as leaders, is responsive. We are here, in leadership of God's people, because we have responded to a summons, because we were sought, called, sent, commissioned by one greater than ourselves that our lives might be expended in work more significant than ourselves."[23]

I am working with a bias of the local congregation being core to the mission of God in the world. Of course, there are other types of ministries that further the *missio Dei*. I am not discounting those. I celebrate the many types of ministries, often engaged in (to reference Ralph Winter's framework again) a sodality type of work. My focus here is on the local congregation, in its many forms.

In this space, pastors hold a key role. And that key role involves not only serving with a sense in a missionary key but also releasing and encouraging the gifts of others, including those with apostolic, prophetic, and evangelistic callings. This will be uncomfortable sometimes. This will mean

22. Neuhaus, *Freedom for Ministry*, 219.

23. Willimon, *Calling and Character*, 16.

giving up control. This will mean levels of uncertainty and even chaos! Pastors must be open to the wild!

Pastoral leaders who serve a local congregation, in line with their particular gift mix, will not be the sole advocates for mission in the broader sense, but rather will work to develop an apostolic imagination for the entire congregation. This new imagination will permeate the pastoral vocation, and this will be evident in daily tasks of pastoral leaders as they nurture a missional focus in the congregation.

Because pastoral leaders are a key component to the missional venture of every local congregation, I offer three metaphors to assist in guiding an understanding of the pastor: pastors as gardeners, as shepherds, as servants.

The Pastor Is a Gardener (a Matter of Character)

Pastors cultivate a life of worship, discipleship, service, and mission. Word and sacrament—Scripture; baptism and Eucharist—define the core identity of a congregation. There is cultivating the soil of a congregation as it develops a missional stance. There is nurturing, watering, fertilizing, pruning, and weeding. The work of a gardener takes patience. This process is slow. It is more like an oak tree than a dandelion.

Pastors want results—fast. But that is not the nature of a garden. Ministry leaders are engaged with those in the congregation as something new emerges. This growth is encouraged more than dictated. While programs are a helpful tool, this cultivation of a missional faith life emerges from below through practices in the midst of the ordinary routines of life and of a faith community.

The idea of gardener moves us beyond the machinelike process that so easily creeps into the church. Our work is more organic, sometimes feeling haphazard, but this is how people grow. Peterson writes,

> The pervasive element in our two-thousand-year pastoral tradition is not someone who "gets things done" but rather the person placed in the community to pay attention and call attention to "what is going on right now" between men and women, with one another and with God—this kingdom of God that is primarily local, relentlessly personal, and prayerful "without ceasing."[24]

24. Peterson, *Pastor*, 5.

I grow roses. Rather, I tend to roses as they grow. I have to let the roses speak to me. I look for over or under watering. I look for pests and mold or lack of nutrients. I prune them so that they will grow well. It all takes time. The work happens over the long haul. This is how the Lord does gardening work in our lives and in our places of ministry. It requires nurture and care and listening and observing. And patience. Willimon writes,

> A major task of Christian ministry is therefore helping our people be open to divine summons and then to have the guts to say yes. No small task in a culture that leads people to believe that they can live unsummoned lives.[25]

This is the call on pastors' lives. And it takes time. It is the work of the gardener. Forming a congregation is a similar type of work. Peterson writes,

> In the mess of work and sin, of families and neighborhoods, my task was to pray and give direction and encourage that lived quality of the gospel—patiently, locally, and personally. Patiently: I would stay with these people; there are no quick or easy ways to do this. Locally: I would embrace the conditions of this place—economics, weather, culture, schools, whatever—so that there would be nothing abstract or piously idealized about what I was doing. Personally: I would know them, know their names, know their homes, know their families, know their work—but I would not pry, I would not treat them as a cause or a project, I would treat them with dignity.[26]

The parable of the sower (Mark 4) reminds us of the work that pastors and other ministry leaders do. They scatter seed in a variety of soils: some hardened, some distracted, some fleeting, some fertile. Part of the pastoral task is to work with these different soils so that the gospel seed might grow. Pastors work and pray to break up the soil that is as hard as asphalt. They weed the soil full of competing plants so that the gospel might take root. They water and nurture tender and vulnerable plants so that they do not wither. They sow seed in new places on the frontier, off the map. And then they trust the Lord with all of our hearts. Jesus notes the mystery of gardening and growth in this parable:

> He also said, "This is what the kingdom of God is like. A man scatters seed on the ground. Night and day, whether he sleeps or gets

25. Willimon, *How Odd of God*, loc. 1480–82 of 4737.

26. Peterson, *Pastor*, 247.

> up, the seed sprouts and grows, though he does not know how. All by itself the soil produces grain—first the stalk, then the head, then the full kernel in the head. As soon as the grain is ripe, he puts the sickle to it, because the harvest has come." (Mark 4:26–29)

Pastoral leaders as gardeners must recall continuously that it is the Lord who brings the harvest.

Pastors demonstrate a mood of humility, patience, and trust in the work of the Spirit in and through a community. It creates a different mood in the congregation. It begins with a new stance for ministry leaders. They are gardeners, not machine operators. Gardeners embrace the seasons of life and, like gardeners, work to create good environments for growth and provide just the right catalysts that will cause new life to emerge. This means giving up control. Pastors are patient with people. People change and grow and fail at various paces, in different seasons. There is an element of trust and surrender.

The pastor as a gardener is a matter of character. A danger in pastoral ministry is taking ourselves too seriously, believing what people say about us. Pastors must guard against a drive toward ego, power, and control. Too many pastors long for celebrity status. It can be intoxicating. It can easily go to one's head. There is a difference between bigness and integrity. Karl Vaters reminds us that bigness is about efficiency, leadership, success, hustle, increase, growth, excitement, effectiveness, passion; while integrity is about love, joy, peace, patience, kindness, goodness, faithfulness, gentleness, self-control.[27] We can debate the nuances, but you get the sense. These two words—"bigness" and "integrity"—offer up two different moods in a congregation.

Ministry leaders must attend to the core of who they are. As they serve as gardeners, they must also receive from the master gardener. Jesus calls all of his followers to abide in him as the vine to the branches. Jesus says,

> I am the true vine, and my Father is the gardener. He cuts off every branch in me that bears no fruit, while every branch that does bear fruit he prunes so that it will be even more fruitful. You are already clean because of the word I have spoken to you. Remain in me, as I also remain in you. No branch can bear fruit by itself; it must remain in the vine. Neither can you bear fruit unless you remain in me.

27. Vaters, *De-Sizing the Church*, 147.

> I am the vine; you are the branches. If you remain in me and I in you, you will bear much fruit; apart from me you can do nothing. If you do not remain in me, you are like a branch that is thrown away and withers; such branches are picked up, thrown into the fire and burned. If you remain in me and my words remain in you, ask whatever you wish, and it will be done for you. This is to my Father's glory, that you bear much fruit, showing yourselves to be my disciples. (John 15:1–8)

Followers of Jesus abide in him. He nurtures his people. He prunes his people so that they might be fruitful, in their own lives and in their ministry. This is true for all believers, and it is critical for ministry leaders. Serving a congregation is a matter of character. Ministry emerges from who the ministry leader is. Ministry leaders demonstrate the fruit of the Spirit. The pastor's work begins here. It the mind-of-Christ attitude:

> Therefore if you have any encouragement from being united with Christ, if any comfort from his love, if any common sharing in the Spirit, if any tenderness and compassion, then make my joy complete by being like-minded, having the same love, being one in spirit and of one mind. Do nothing out of selfish ambition or vain conceit. Rather, in humility value others above yourselves, not looking to your own interests but each of you to the interests of the others. (Phil 2:1–4)

In your relationships with one another, have the same mindset as Christ Jesus:

> Who, being in very nature God, did not consider equality with God something to be used to his own advantage; rather, he made himself nothing by taking the very nature of a servant. (Phil 2:6–7)

This is living by the cross; it is a crucified ministry. Pastors follow the example of Jesus in John 13. Jesus took a towel and a basin and stooped before his disciples. He showed them how to serve. Jesus drove the point home:

> Jesus called them together and said, "You know that those who are regarded as rulers of the Gentiles lord it over them, and their high officials exercise authority over them. Not so with you. Instead, whoever wants to become great among you must be your servant, and whoever wants to be first must be slave of all. For even the Son of Man did not come to be served, but to serve, and to give his life as a ransom for many." (Mark 10:42–45)

Not so with you! Those are the words we need to hear over and over as we walk in our pastoral vocation. We are tempted to be people driven by ambition. While we must not be mediocre, and we must do our work well, the underlying mood of our lives must be the cross.

My default mode for life, for leading and for ministry, was that of a motorboat. This grew out of a sense of frustration and impatience, along with my natural inclinations. I wanted things to move and change. And I wanted this to happen fast! I would power up and move toward my predetermined goal. In the process, I would run over swimmers, buoys, and anything in my way. If there was a plan, I would amp it up. "This is what God wants for our church. So here we go. Get on board, or get out of the way." That did not work as well as I had imagined. Matters got done quickly, but people got hurt. Soon, ministry stalled. I had to ask for forgiveness along the way.

A better path for ministry is that of a sailboat. Sailing can still have goals and objectives, but they are less precise. These objectives might change based on circumstances and new insights. Sailing is subject to winds, waves, and currents. Sometimes sailing means moving forward fast. Other times, one is becalmed. It's all part of sailing.

The Spirit of God is in the midst of the people of God. Pastors should not go off to the mountaintop, receive the vision, and then come back to the people and share what "the pastor" received. God is at work in the church in greater ways and beyond just the pastor. Church leaders certainly help to enable visions and missional imaginations, but church leaders need to listen to the people of God in a local congregation, hearing what the Lord is saying to them. Hopes and vision emerges from that dialogue. It is a slower process. Sailing is slower than powerboating, but the result is more enduring and healthier. And it is the people of God, in a local setting, doing the work together. The Lord speaks to the church gathered, not just the lead pastor. The Lord works through the whole church, not just the pastor. This requires a shift in the understanding of the role of the pastor, and it requires a shift in heart. Humility. This is a matter of character.

Pastors as gardeners recognize the power and status that come with their role but hold that in check through cultivating an ongoing life of humility. Pastors are to be transparent, vulnerable, and accountable. This sense of humility then becomes a greater reality in the life of a congregation. It leads a congregation to mission. Paul expresses it this way:

> For we know, brothers and sisters loved by God, that he has chosen you, because our gospel came to you not simply with words but also with power, with the Holy Spirit and deep conviction. You know how we lived among you for your sake. You became imitators of us and of the Lord, for you welcomed the message in the midst of severe suffering with the joy given by the Holy Spirit. And so you became a model to all the believers in Macedonia and Achaia. (1 Thess 1:4–7)

A gardener is intentional. Jim Collins writes about leadership as a blending of personal humility and professional will.[28] This type of leader demonstrates modesty and seeks to create superb results. This person acts with quiet determination and demonstrates unwavering resolve. This leader channels ambition into mission and also sets the standard for advancement. This type of leader looks in the mirror and takes responsibility and looks out the window to give credit.

The Pastor Is a Shepherd (a Matter of Competence)

Pastors care for people in their congregation and empower them to serve. The idea of the shepherd is a good corrective to celebrity pastors. Pastors are shepherds. (The image of the shepherd is found throughout Scripture, in the Old Testament [e.g., Ps 23; Isa 40:11; Ezek 34] as well as in the ministry of Jesus [e.g., Matt 15:24; Luke 12:32].) The New Testament specifically uses this metaphor to describe leaders in the church (e.g., John 21:16; Acts 20:28–29; Eph 4:11; Jude 12; Heb 13:20; 1 Pet 2:25). This is the call on pastors' lives from 1 Pet 5:

> To the elders among you, I appeal as a fellow elder and a witness of Christ's sufferings who also will share in the glory to be revealed: Be shepherds of God's flock that is under your care, watching over them—not because you must, but because you are willing, as God wants you to be; not pursuing dishonest gain, but eager to serve; not lording it over those entrusted to you, but being examples to the flock. And when the Chief Shepherd appears, you will receive the crown of glory that will never fade away.
>
> In the same way, you who are younger, submit yourselves to your elders. All of you, clothe yourselves with humility toward one another, because,

28. Collins, *Good to Great*, 17–22.

> "God opposes the proud
> but shows favor to the humble."
>
> Humble yourselves, therefore, under God's mighty hand, that he may lift you up in due time. Cast all your anxiety on him because he cares for you. (1 Pet 5:1–7)

Pastors are shepherds accountable to the Chief Shepherd and to each other in humility. Pastors are not simply shepherds, but "under shepherds" in apprenticeship to the risen Christ, the Chief Shepherd.[29] Shepherds nurture and lead; they guide and protect. Shepherds watch carefully over their sheep. As Peter says, they should do so willingly, even eagerly. Peter appeals to Christian leaders as one who has witnessed firsthand both the suffering of Jesus and his resurrection to new life. When he writes to persecuted Christians, he doesn't dwell on the present, but on the future. Hang in there, he says, because for the faithful, the best is yet to come. Be faithful under shepherds, and do so gladly, knowing that when the Chief Shepherd returns, you will share in his glory. As Professor Thomas Oden says,

> The vocation of a pastor is to know the parish territory, its dangers, its green meadows, its steep precipices, its seasons and its possibilities. The pastor leads the flock to spring water and safe vegetables. The flock recognizes their own good through the shepherd's voice. They do not see it in their interest to follow strangers. They know their own shepherd will not mislead them. The shepherd is able to anticipate their needs in advance and is willing to deal with each one individually.[30]

Shepherding is hard, unglamorous work. Pastors, like shepherds, sacrificially give themselves away. What sustains them in this life of service? Shepherds do hard work. They don't simply sit back and tend sheep. They are fierce workers. Lesslie Newbigin uses the phrase "warrior shepherds."[31] They proactively nurture a flock to good pastures, lead it forward, and protect against wolves and other perils (Acts 20:17–38).

Pastors are professionals in ministry. As pastors shepherd congregations, they must do so with competence. Lives are entrusted to their care. Pastors earn degrees in order to serve well. Pastors become credentialed.

29. Oden, *Pastoral Theology*, 51.

30. Oden, *Pastoral Theology*, 52.

31. Newbigin, *Good Shepherd*, 14.

They are held to a level of accountability. They are expected to live up to high standards of conduct.

Professionals such as physicians, lawyers, teachers, and ministers are people who have received specialized formal education, are credentialed by some public standard, and abide by a code of conduct. As professionals, pastors should engage in lifelong theological education and training for the practice of ministry. Pastors are expected to be competent, "capable of leading wisely and of providing particular services to the community."[32]

The perception of the pastorate as a profession must never be allowed to overshadow its nature as a calling from God. Ministry is not merely a profession; ministry is also a vocation. Ministers are more than those who are credentialed and validated by the approval of their fellow members of their profession; they are also called by God.[33] This is a divine appointment. That should cause pastors to pause and consider the weight of this calling. Pastors sense the call in their lives. This call is affirmed by those around them as ministry gifts are practiced. This call is often confirmed through a formal process such as licensure or ordination.

This professional role equips pastors to serve well—to preach the word, to invite people to worship God, to provide leadership in a congregation, to comfort and care. Pastors offer healing, not harm, to those in a congregation. They should be both learned and competent. The vast majority of pastors want to serve well and desire the knowledge and skills needed for effective ministry.

But a pastor is more than what the world would characterize as a professional, at least by modern definitions. We need to get back to the earlier sense of a professional as one who professes, because this is the core of the pastorate. As Willimon puts it, "We have degraded 'professionals' by making them primarily people who *know* something that the rest of us do not, rather than being people who the rest of us *are* not."[34] Pastors should live more as amateurs rather than professionals. Amateurs operate out of a different motivation than professionals. The word "amateur" comes from the Latin *amare*: to love. That is the intrinsic motivation, doing something for the love of it.[35]

32. Jones and Armstrong, *Resurrecting Excellence*, loc. 1097 of 2425.

33. Willimon, *Calling and Character*, 33. See also Niebuhr, *Purpose of the Church*, 64.

34. Willimon, *Calling and Character*, 32; emphasis added.

35. Shirky, *Cognitive Surplus*, 82.

This professional characterization of the clergy is a primary way ministry leaders see themselves, but there is a danger here. Pastors are professionals, at least in a North American culture, but pastors must guard against a sense of professionalization. Churches too easily can be seen as businesses or organizational machines, particularly as they grow beyond the face-to-face relationships of smaller congregations. This can disrupt the missional nature of a congregation. The pastor becomes less of an apostle, a priest, or a teacher, and more of a CEO. A congregation can too easily fall into a rigid, bureaucratic stance that stifles innovation and creativity.

We must guard against the "pastor as expert" mentality. While the pastor has professional knowledge, we must not allow the pastor to be seen as expert with the "techniques" and "strategies" for matters concerning church. Alan Roxburgh comments that the Spirit of God is among the people of God.[36] The Spirit is not the possession of the pastor. The Spirit does not speak only to the pastor. This idea of pastor as expert leads to a disengaged laity. It undercuts the priesthood of all believers. It creates a bottleneck in the church. It feeds the pastor's ego.

The church as organization needs to function well, but ministry leaders must intentionally resist a move toward institutionalization. Organizational structures are important to the ongoing work of a congregation, and it is better to be intentional about them. While structures are necessary for the church, institutionalization as a key feature of the modern church must be resisted. Pastors and leadership structures can inhibit the move of the Spirit. No present structure must be seen as ultimate. The presence and power of the Spirit are always primary. Pastors must guide and guard their congregations with discernment. At the same time, they must not use their position as pastor to dominate and control.

Pastors as professionals are susceptible to market forces and competition. Pastors become the vendors of religious goods and services. Pastors become marketers, and the congregation becomes consumers. We are no longer disciples but customers who need to be pleased. Peterson expresses it this way:

> There is also this to be said. North American culture does not offer congenial conditions in which to live vocationally as a pastor. Men and women who are pastors in America today find that they have entered into a way of life that is in ruins. The vocation of pastor

36. See this idea in Roxburgh, *Missional*; Roxburgh, "Attend to What's Happening"; Love, "Discerning God's Calling."

> has been replaced by the strategies of religious entrepreneurs with business plans. Any kind of continuity with pastors in times past is virtually nonexistent. We are a generation that feels as if it is having to start out from scratch to figure out a way to represent and nurture this richly nuanced and all-involving life of Christ in a country that "knew not Joseph."[37]

Pastors advance the missional nature of the church and must not get caught up in institutionalization of ministry. Alan Hirsch describes the difference between a missional movement and institutional religion. An organic missional movement has a pioneering sense as its central role. These movements advocate for change with a look toward the future. They tend to be mobile and dynamic. Institutional religion, on the other hand, is a more centralized structure that tends toward being static and fixed. There is desire to preserve the past.[38] Of course there are more extreme polarities, but do you get a sense of the difference and the dangers?

The pastor as a professional has the danger of distancing pastors from their people. Pastors are to engage with others. They get their hands dirty. They are not stuck, isolated in an office. Pastors are with their people, in the community, at coffee shops, at church social events, and at workdays. As Pope Francis says, we are to be "shepherds living with 'the smell of the sheep.' This I ask you: be shepherds, with the 'smell of the sheep,' make it real, as shepherds among your flock, fishers of men."[39] Eugene Peterson puts the role of the pastor in perspective:

> I'd tell them that pastoring is not a very glamorous job. It's a very taking-out-the-laundry and changing-the-diapers kind of job. And I think I would try to disabuse them of any romantic ideas of what it is. As a pastor, you've got to be willing to take people as they are. And live with them where they are. And not impose your will on them. Because God has different ways of being with people, and you don't always know what they are.[40]

Pastors, therefore, are those who do not merely look to increase their professional competence, as useful as this may be. They intentionally reflect on their ministry and ask, "Where are the presence and power of God being manifested in this congregation's life, in my life, and in my pastoral

37. Peterson, *Pastor*, 4.
38. Hirsch, *Forgotten Ways*, 339.
39. Francis, *Smell of the Sheep*, loc. 297–98.
40. Peterson, "Faithful to the End," para. 6.

leadership?"[41] Thus, while being a professional is an important aspect of pastoral work, we must guard against distortions of the role. Pastors can get so caught up in the profession that the ministry becomes a mere job or career. Again, Peterson writes,

> A job is an assignment to do work that can be quantified and evaluated. It is pretty easy to decide whether a job has been completed or not. It is pretty easy to tell whether a job is done well or badly. But a vocation is not a job in that sense. I can be hired to do a job, paid a fair wage if I do it, dismissed if I don't. But I can't be hired to be a pastor, for my primary responsibility is not to the people I serve but to the God I serve.[42]

Peterson notes the difference between "running a church" and "care of souls." Running a church involves initiative. It is taking charge, taking responsibility. It asks, "What do we do?" Care of souls is about developing a cultivated awareness of the reality that God has already taken the initiative. It asks, "What has God been up to?"[43]

Running a church is about getting things done. Care of souls is getting to the heart of things: who these people are and what they are becoming. Running a church is about solving problems. Care of souls sees life and people as mysteries to be explored. See the difference? The ministry stance creates, over time, a mood—a healthy mood—in the congregation.

As a job, the ministry demands much; it takes its toll and saps the spirit. Exhausted or disillusioned pastors lose their passion; the vitality drains out of their witness and leadership. They find themselves simply going through the motions of worship, preaching, and the tasks of ministry. They become aloof and isolated. When profession routinely supersedes call in the pastor's imagination, the life of ministry can become hollow and empty.

And congregations don't make it easier. Pastors know the competing expectations of what the pastor thinks is most important and what the pastor feels called to do. These conflicting expectations are a great source of stress and discouragement. The fact that most of the pastor's work is hidden makes the task even more difficult. We know and cringe at this too-typical job description:

41. Jones and Armstrong, *Resurrecting Excellence*, loc. 145 of 2425.

42. Peterson, *Pastor*, 165.

43. See Peterson Center, "Holy Presence"; Peterson, *Contemplative Pastor*; Senkbeil, *Care of Souls*.

> WANTED: Person to fill position that involves important but undervalued work; exact job description unclear. Long hours; must work weekends. Master's degree required; doctorate preferred. Must be accomplished at multitasking, including running an organization without clear authority to do so. The successful candidate will be skilled as a public speaker, manager, politician, and therapist, and will devote significant time each week to pastoral visits. The position reports to multiple bosses.[44]

And wouldn't it be wonderful as a pastor-professional to work in environments with this type of job description:

> WANTED: Persons for a vocation that leads God's people in bearing witness to God's new creation revealed in Jesus Christ by the power of the Holy Spirit. Work schedule is shaped by relationships, focusing on what is important in people's lives, and depends on regular rhythms of work, rest, and play. Compensation is shaped by a mutual discernment of what is necessary in order for the persons (and, where appropriate, their families) to have an appropriately well-lived life. The vocation involves cultivating holy dispositions, preaching and teaching, nurturing rigorous study, and shaping practices of faithful living in church and world. Lifelong education and formation [are] expected in order to enable others also to grow throughout their lives. The successful candidate will collaborate with others towards the same ends. The vocation reports to God.[45]

Pastors Occupy an Office (So They Must Be Servants)

Seeing pastoral ministry as an office highlights the pastor's authority as a representative of Jesus Christ in and for a community. Pastors, especially those from less liturgical traditions, may recoil from this sense of office and authority. But it is important to recognize that those in pastoral positions represent something larger than themselves. Some call this gravitas. Pastor Craig Barnes writes,

> The old Pietists used to write in their journals about gravitas. It was their description of a soul that had gained enough weightiness to be attractive, like all things with a gravitational pull. Most people

44. Jones and Armstrong, *Resurrecting Excellence*, loc. 387 of 2425.

45. Jones and Armstrong, *Resurrecting Excellence*, loc. 387 of 2425.

> can immediately think about someone in their lives who has this gravitas. Maybe it's a former teacher, coach, grandparent, boss, the woman down the street who happily interrupts her gardening to speak with you . . . or a really good pastor. How does the soul of a pastor become well formed in a calling that can just as easily suck it dry as fill it with gravitas? The best way to answer that question is by telling a story and pointing, as if to say "remember that moment when . . ." something holy happened to me. No pastor can pry those moments from God's hand, but an attentive one can behold them. And in the beholding, the pastor's soul is formed.[46]

This is a derivative authority. It is an authority contingent on one's stewardship of the trust of the office. Pastors are people with authority but under authority.

One of the best examples of office I found is in an episode of the television show *West Wing*. In the episode "Take This Sabbath Day," United States President Jed Bartlet struggled to make a decision whether or not to commute the sentence of a person who was going to be executed. After a day of meeting with advisors, he decided to let the execution take place. As the midnight hour of the execution approached, he met with his family priest in the Oval Office. In the interaction with his priest, Bartlet had the priest refer to him as Mr. President, and he called the priest by his first name. After he received word that the execution had taken place, realizing the moral weight of his decision, the roles changed. Bartlet referred to the priest as Father, and the priest referred to the president as Jed.[47]

The office of pastor is a space larger than any one person. Pastors enter into that space realizing the power and authority that they have, holding that power for the good of others. This is a sacred trust, requiring diligence and thoughtfulness on the part of conscientious pastors. Pastors live into something beyond who we are. The task is more than we are able to accomplish. This is a key aspect of the pastor's work that must be recognized to avoid its misuse.

There is a sacramental sense to the work that pastors do. Pastors are broken, imperfect, and very human vessels. And yet the Lord uses them. Paul writes,

> Therefore, since through God's mercy we have this ministry, we do not lose heart. Rather, we have renounced secret and shameful

46. Barnes, *Diary of Pastor's Soul*, 11.

47. Sorkin, "Take This Sabbath Day."

> ways; we do not use deception, nor do we distort the word of God. On the contrary, by setting forth the truth plainly we commend ourselves to everyone's conscience in the sight of God. . . . For what we preach is not ourselves, but Jesus Christ as Lord, and ourselves as your servants for Jesus' sake. . . . But we have this treasure in jars of clay to show that this all-surpassing power is from God and not from us. We are hard pressed on every side, but not crushed; perplexed, but not in despair; persecuted, but not abandoned; struck down, but not destroyed. We always carry around in our body the death of Jesus, so that the life of Jesus may also be revealed in our body. For we who are alive are always being given over to death for Jesus' sake, so that his life may also be revealed in our mortal body. So then, death is at work in us, but life is at work in you. (2 Cor 4:1–12)

Pastors carry great responsibility for their people. Pastors must not take this responsibility lightly. Pastoral theologian Ray S. Anderson notes the power and influence pastors hold when he writes,

> Whether we realize it or not, every act of ministry reveals something of God. By act of ministry I mean a sermon preached, a lesson taught, a marriage performed, counsel offered, any other word or act that people might construe as carrying God's blessing, warning, or judgment.[48]

What pastors—ministry leaders—say and do matters. Words and actions carry a good amount of weight.

I serve as a volunteer police chaplain in my town. One Sunday after church, I was called to the hospital because the child of one of the officers had nearly drowned. The child survived but with severe brain damage. Weeks later, I was walking the halls of the police station and ran into the officer. He stopped me and asked a question: "Where was God when my child was at the bottom of the pool?" Whatever I said, theologically correct or not, sensitive or insensitive, right or wrong, became the word of God at that moment to him and to his family. There is a weight to our words. There is a weight to our presence.

When a freight train slammed into a commuter train, killing twenty-nine residents in our community, I was called upon to lead a memorial service one week after the tragedy and again one year later. I was acting as

48. R. Anderson, *Soul of Ministry*, 7.

a pastor for the community. My role was bigger than me. I was helping to bring the collective sorrow and anger of a community before the Lord.

Pastors are just people! Ordinary. Nothing unique. Again, we believe in the priesthood of all believers. And pastors should be working hard to empower people in their congregations to use their gifts in all types of ministries. Still, many in our culture "send for the priest," so to speak, in times of trouble. While I was serving as a youth pastor, a friend of mine fell off a roof and was badly hurt. He was rushed to the hospital, and the church gathered around him. I offered comfort and prayers, as did others. But when the senior pastor walked into the room, there was a shared sense that the *real* prayer powerhouse had arrived!

This is not an unusual scenario. How many hospitalized church members have complained of being ignored by "the church," not because their brothers and sisters haven't come to pray with them, but because the *senior pastor* hasn't visited? In some cases, not even the associate will do. This is not, of course, the proper response; theologically, it is simply wrong. And pastors can work to change this response over time. But meanwhile, they must take seriously the fact that they are the representatives of God to their congregations.

This is the office of pastor. It usually includes the gifting of pastor, but it is broader than this. The office of pastor is a more formal recognition by a local congregation, ministry, or denomination. And it is also an informal recognition by those being cared for and served. This office of pastor represents something bigger than the individual. It is an ascribed identity. Theologian John Weborg from North Park Theological Seminary notes the difference between an achieved identity and an ascribed identity. An achieved identity is something I have earned. I earned a master of divinity degree. I paid tuition; I did the work. I earned the degree. But ordination is different. It is an ascribed identity. The larger church is the custodian of this identity. It affirms my vocational calling, but the ordination is not mine. But the church that ordained me can revoke my ordination and remove my stole. The church, not I, is the custodian of my ordination. Thus, pastoral officeholders are persons with authority but under authority.[49]

The pastoral office bears witness to Jesus and to the in-breaking of God's kingdom. As representatives of Jesus Christ, pastors strive toward holiness. Though all followers of Christ are to imitate him, the pastor is to

49. See Weborg, *Made Healthy in Ministry*, loc. 1094–95, 1114–15.

be an exemplary person, "adorning . . . the gospel with a holy life."[50] All of this is true, despite the fact that pastors have their own struggles in trying the best they can to follow the ways of Christ. Pastors do not come to the role having been fully formed in the faith. Rather, they are shaped over time, through obedience to God's call, in the midst of day-to-day interactions with ordinary congregations.

Those who occupy the office of pastor must be people of integrity. Pastors have a power that can spiritually, emotionally, and physically harm others, creating an environment of toxic faith. Ezekiel 34 speaks harshly about the false shepherds, those with authority.

Being a servant is a good corrective to the sense of pastor as office. Paul uses the most tender language to describe his role as servant:

> You know we never used flattery, nor did we put on a mask to cover up greed—God is our witness. We were not looking for praise from people, not from you or anyone else, even though as apostles of Christ we could have asserted our authority. Instead, we were like young children among you. Just as a nursing mother cares for her children, so we cared for you. Because we loved you so much, we were delighted to share with you not only the gospel of God but our lives as well. Surely you remember, brothers and sisters, our toil and hardship; we worked night and day in order not to be a burden to anyone while we preached the gospel of God to you. You are witnesses, and so is God, of how holy, righteous and blameless we were among you who believed. For you know that we dealt with each of you as a father deals with his own children, encouraging, comforting and urging you to live lives worthy of God, who calls you into his kingdom and glory. (1 Thess 2:5–12)

Paul lived this out in his life and in his ministry. His ministry grew out of a sense of humble trust in Jesus:

> Therefore, in order to keep me from becoming conceited, I was given a thorn in my flesh, a messenger of Satan, to torment me. Three times I pleaded with the Lord to take it away from me. But he said to me, "My grace is sufficient for you, for my power is made perfect in weakness." Therefore, I will boast all the more gladly about my weaknesses, so that Christ's power may rest on me. That is why, for Christ's sake, I delight in weaknesses, in insults, in hardships, in persecutions, in difficulties. For when I am weak, then I am strong. (2 Cor 12:7–10)

50. Neuhaus, *Freedom for Ministry*, 210.

Pastors and other ministry leaders play a key role in provoking and encouraging a missional mood within a congregation. Pastors can be a bottleneck to a sent type of mission, or pastors can be a gateway that cultivates a different mood within a congregation—for the good of the congregation and the good of the neighborhood. Pastors are gardeners, shepherds, and servants. They are called to this work. They serve as shepherds in a local place caring for the congregation and sending the congregation out for the good of the neighborhood and beyond. And, they are ambassadors of good news, representatives of the good gospel within the congregation and beyond.

Eugene Peterson tells a story about the wonderful Jewish writer Chaim Potok. As he went off to college, his mother said, "Chaim, I know you want to be a writer, but I have a better idea. Why don't you become a brain surgeon. You will keep a lot of people from dying; you'll make a lot of money." But Chaim said, "No, Mama, I want to be a writer." At every opportunity—vacation breaks, meetings, family meals—his mother would continue to push for a "better idea" while Chaim would insist that he wants "to be a writer." Eventually, the pressure intensified, and Chaim's mother became insistent: "Chaim, you're wasting your time. Be a brain surgeon, you will keep people from dying." Chaim exploded, "Mama, I don't want to keep people from dying, I want to show them how to live!"[51]

"I want to show people how to live." This is what it means to be a pastor. This is the conviction that captures your heart.

51. Peterson, *Under the Unpredictable Plant*, 46.

4

How

The local church must act differently than it has in the past. It is insanity to keep doing church the old way, as good as that was, and expecting a different outcome. When the reality of a changed world is defined and accepted, something new can emerge with the right catalysts, key practices, and a sense of trust, hope, and patience. Rather than setting out with a programmatic goal with defined outcomes, this shift occurs by reimagining the local church as a missional congregation. These new missional forms of church are provoked and disturbed, not directed.

Faith communities are not transformed through strategic plans that move a congregation from where it is to an intended future. Congregations do not follow a linear path from A to B; rather, the life of a congregation is cyclical.[1] They move and change organically through various seasons. The end result is not clear or certain. At the core, this is the work of the Holy Spirit. It is the Lord who brings about any transformation of a congregation and our lives. The Lord is at work. The Lord is always out before us, moving, shaping, and urging. Our task is to discern where the Lord is at work, surrender our lives and our work to the Lord, and join the Lord in this ongoing work. New Testament scholar James D. G. Dunn says the Spirit at work in us "transcends human ability and transforms human inability."[2] This

1. Dallas Willard writes, "What we most learn in his yoke, beyond acting with him, is to abandon outcomes to God, accepting that we do not have in ourselves—in our own 'heart, soul, mind, and strength'—the wherewithal to make this come out right, whatever 'this' is" (*Renovation of the Heart*, loc. 4272).

2. McKnight and Barringer, *Pivot*, 189. See Dunn, *Acts of the Apostles*, 5.

chapter is about creating an environment in the local church that fosters a new missional stance as a sent congregation.

The task of missional leaders is to provoke and catalyze existing structures so that something new might emerge. This requires a new imagination. Something new, something yet to be determined and maybe even imagined, is developed through a heartfelt ache, a burning desire, and a hope for something new.

This is a different way of nurturing change. It has been said, "If you want to build a ship, don't drum up people to collect wood and don't assign them tasks and work, but rather teach them to long for the endless immensity of the sea."[3] This is not about strategies or long-range goals. Rather, ministry leaders are creating an environment where new imaginations and ecclesial practices can emerge.

The current church systems are becoming obsolete. Ministry leaders are too often trained in seminary for a world that no longer exists. These systems once worked well. Many loved those old forms. Nostalgically, we hold onto those forms of being church. The church systems of the day are perfectly designed for our current ways of doing church, but the world changed! Alan Hirsch reminds us of "an axiom of organizational theory—that we are perfectly designed to achieve what we are currently achieving."[4]

Rubem Alves writes, "We know dinosaurs only by their bones. The largest, most powerful animals to walk the earth are extinct. Their 'arrogance of power' was of no use. . . . The dinosaurs disappeared not because they were too weak, but because they were too strong. Their fantastic power came from a biological framework which was basically absurd, and the result was annihilation."[5] Could it be that the contemporary church is in a similar situation? A danger in the church is hubris. We think we are indestructible, too big to fail, or that our church is different from others. Churches resist change; it is better, safer, or more theologically correct to stay as the church is. The idolatry to a current method leads to extinction because we cannot adapt.

Alvin Toffler writes in *Future Shock*, "The illiterate of the future are not those who can't read or write but those who cannot learn, unlearn, and

3. Commonly attributed to Antoine de Saint-Exupéry. See quoteresearch, "Teach Them to Yearn."

4. Hirsch, 5Q, loc. 3506–7 of 5907. Willard writes, "Your system is perfectly designed to yield the result you are getting" (*Divine Conspiracy*, 58).

5. Alves, *Tomorrow's Child*, 1.

relearn."[6] That needs to be our sense again today, in our changing culture. We need the spirit of the church in Antioch. Church structures must change in order to meet new challenges. Church systems cannot be static. The old ways of doing church no longer work. Sending congregations must move off the map into uncharted and unknown territory. Congregations are not machines; they are gardens. Congregations are nurtured into something new, yet to be discovered.

The world has changed. The location of the church in the world is different. The church is no longer the center of culture. We are in diaspora. The old ways of being church will never come back, as much as we want this to be true. As much as we attempt this, it won't happen. So we must change. The love of Christ compels us.

This is a time of liminality, a time of transition. Pastor and missiologist Alan Roxburgh notes that the church is moving through a transition from a period of stability where the world is predictable and known to a period that is unknown and uncertain. In this in-between, in the transition period, the church experiences discontinuous change. Roxburgh calls this the great unraveling. It is quite unnerving.[7] Pastor and professor Tod Bolsinger highlights what's at stake for leaders in their experience of conflict: "The real challenge of leadership is not tactical or strategic but emotional. Not only do we have to deal with the inner uncertainty that goes with leading into uncharted territory, but we also have to manage the two-front battle, which includes our own need to be liked, to gain approval from others or to be seen as a competent professional. And sometimes we get really anxious that we are never going to measure up."[8]

Change brings a sense of loss. It is hard. My kids have grown up. I love their life now, but I miss the old days. I think we were good parents when our kids were young. We can't parent them the same way now. I like the way church was when I was growing up, even when I was pastoring a congregation. I feel nostalgic about it. Church has been the center of my entire life. And yet change is necessary. The gospel compels us to do our work in new ways.

6. Toffler, *Future Shock*, 414.

7. Roxburgh, *Joining God, Remaking Church*, 21.

8. Bolsinger, *Canoeing the Mountains*, 136–37. See also Hayden, *Remissioning Church*, 187. Hayden's book is a good summary of adaptive change; Bolsinger's book is an excellent resource.

Like the Israelites, sometimes it feels better to go back to Egypt than to wander in the wilderness. Egypt is known. The wilderness is uncertain. Moving into the wilderness creates a sense of loss and along with it fear and anger. All this causes disruption! It is easier to stay in Egypt. When you leave the promised land and start out, it is disruptive and scary. The old ways, though not perfect, are at least familiar. It's easy to go back. But there is an idolatry attached to old forms. We get caught up in them. They become sacred cows. Insanity is doing the same thing over and over and expecting a different result.

The great danger is that we get stuck. All organizations tend toward institutionalization, a preoccupation with itself and drive for self-preservation. A diminishing passion for innovation and mission is the consequence. Richard Rohr notes that organizations shift from the man to the movement to the machine to the monument to memory.[9] Religious organizations are categorized as institutionalized when the organizational practices of that body are seen as a set of "taken for granted" processes, and the organization itself is seen as legitimate in accordance with dominant norms and values.[10] This routinization of the organization leads to a sense of legitimacy for like-structured organizations and a sense of illegitimacy and suspicion for those who exist outside of the established structures.[11]

Seeing ministry as a garden, not a machine, changes how we do ministry. Peterson writes,

> Congregation is the topsoil in pastoral work. This is the material substance in which all the Spirit's work takes place—these people, assembled in worship, dispersed in blessing. They are so ordinary, so unobtrusively there; it is easy to take them for granted, quit seeing the interactive energies, and become so preoccupied in building my theological roads, mission constructs, and parking lot curricula that I start treating this precious congregational topsoil as something dead and inert, to be rearranged to suit my vision, and then to bulldoze whatever isn't immediately useful to the sidelines where it won't interfere with my projects. But this is the field of pastoral work, just as it is, teeming with energy, nutrients, mixing death and life. I cannot manufacture it, but I can protect it. I can nourish it. I can refrain from polluting or violating it. But mostly, like the farmer with his topsoil, I must respect and honor

9. Rohr, *Hope Against Darkness*, 75.

10. Packard, "Organizational Structure, Religious Belief," 12.

11. DiMaggio, "Relevance of Organization Theory," 14.

> and reverence it, be in awe before the vast mysteries contained in its unassuming ordinariness.[12]

The church is a garden. We must resist the culture that sees the church as a machine. A machine is efficient. A machine speaks to progress, forward movement. The church in our day has taken on the characteristics of a fast-food restaurant; Professor John Drane has utilized the work of George Ritzer to demonstrate how the American church has uncritically become "McDonaldized."

Drane outlines the primary traits of McDonaldization:

> *Efficiency*: Seeking the quick and efficient fix to spiritual difficulties or congregational issues. Pragmatism triumphs in the modern church.
>
> *Calculability*: The number game, stresses what can be counted: converts to the faith, or at least to this church, size of a budget, number of people on staff, the number who attend worship, the size and magnificence of buildings. If it is growing, progressing, expanding, the church is a success.
>
> *Predictability*: Speaks to the standardization of religious activities from worship patterns, to political and social makeup, to moral values and choices.
>
> *Control*: Power is evident throughout the church from the assigning of tasks and roles, to the organization of groups and committees, to the subject of sermons and the opportunities for dialogue and debate.[13]

Pragmatic concerns play heavily in the McDonaldized church. Roxburgh notes "technique is the primary method for reestablishing the church's place in culture. God is but a legitimating footnote of ecclesiology."[14] Something is good if it works. All is well if attendance numbers and contributions are up. If these markers are rising, God must be blessing. David Bosch writes, "The gospel could be reduced to information that was to be conveyed in what was perceived to be the most efficient way possible. The key problem to be solved was to find the right methods and techniques and

12. Peterson, *Under the Unpredictable Plant*, 134–35.

13. Drane, *McDonaldization of the Church*.

14. Roxburgh, *Missionary Congregation, Leadership, Liminality*, 20.

to organize a campaign, crusade or drive. This put a premium on program rather than the formation of a community of disciples."[15]

The modern church has embraced the McDonaldized forms of church. Even a cursory look at the American church illustrates the pervasiveness of McDonaldization. Church success is measured by numbers—worship attendance, conversions and baptisms, size of staff, seating capacities. Church leaders are quick to pick up the latest book or resource that will advance the church through the application of the newly developed program. The church growth movement, especially in its American expression, has been in danger of applying Ritzer's dynamics uncritically in the quest for numerical growth. As churches adopt a business model for congregational life, pastors become marketers of programs and services, falling into the religious vendor mode serving the religious consumer. The recent multisite movement unabashedly speaks in franchise terms. Could this be the last gasp of the modern church?

The local congregation must break the McDonaldization mindset. It creeps into the church in so many ways. We judge our success by the same metrics used in the business world. We develop our own sense of value as a congregation and as ministry leaders by those measures of success. We are defeated, discouraged, and anxious when we don't meet the mark.

The love of Christ compels us toward a new way of being church and relating to each other and to our neighbor. We are sent, not settled. But it is hard. I have had countless times of being discouraged. I work hard. Our church works hard. And yet it seems that the going is so slow. I would hear the success stories from others. I would get jealous and even more discouraged. I would try to copy what they were doing, but it didn't seem to work for us. Can these bones live? I had my doubts. Dry bones everywhere. It simply gets very, very tough.

Gardening is different. It moves according to seasons. Seasons of growth. Seasons of being fallow. Gardening sets expectations based on these seasons and factors like water, weather, pests, or disease. All of these are factored into the gardening process. The basis for evaluation changes. And, to some degree, the gardener is not in control. In the garden, growth cannot be dictated. Instead, it is nurtured, cultivated, discerned, and corrected.

Gardening requires cultivation and pruning. It is a different way to look at an organization, a local congregation. New life emerges because of careful gardening. My family now lives in Colorado. It has a very different

15. Bosch, *Believing in the Future*, 62.

growing season. In California, the growing season was nearly year-round. My garden flourished every season. Now in Colorado, the growth cycle is different. In spring, plants begin to emerge. They flourish in spring and summer. By fall, leaves begin to change and plants begin to go dormant. By winter, the plants turn to sticks and are covered in snow. It looks like there is no life. But the cycle begins again. With spring, there is the promise of something new. Grasses emerge first, then leaves, and then perennials again. This is the cycle of life. Not a machine. A garden.

This is a different way of looking at a local congregation on mission. It is not forced. It is not dictated. Rather, an environment is nurtured that allows something new to emerge. A congregation discovers a new path of mission as a new mood is nurtured within that congregation. This process is slower. It takes time. It is based on trust, which can be developed only over time. The church, every local congregation, is a pilgrim people. There is a sense of movement about us.

This is not frantic activity (like when I am lost, I just start driving faster and crazier). Rather, the church on mission, never content, is always extending itself—to each other and out into the community. The church is a safe haven, a worshipping community. It pushes forward in ways that are unique to that congregation. The gospel gets lived out in every congregation by real people! Newbigin reminds us,

> How is it possible that the gospel should be credible, that people should come to believe that the power which has the last word in human affairs is represented by a man hanging on a cross? I am suggesting that the only answer, the only hermeneutic of the gospel, is a congregation of men and women who believe it and live by it.[16]

Too often I lived by my own effort to come up with the formula, adopt the latest technique, and watch the growth unfold. It is never that easy. This is church-as-machine thinking. We need to move to a new stance. Andrew Root and Blair Bertrand, in *When the Church Stops Working*, call us to a new way of being the church. It promotes a Sabbath mindset. It means learning to let go, allowing the Lord to do a new work. We stop striving. We move beyond strategies and programs and goals. Rather, the current system is provoked as a new environment is nurtured so that something new might emerge. Something that is off the map. That we don't plan! I am reminded of Paul's words:

16. Newbigin, *Gospel in Pluralist Society*, 227.

> I planted the seed, Apollos watered it, but God has been making it grow. So neither the one who plants nor the one who waters is anything, but only God, who makes things grow. (1 Cor 3:6–7)

It's God who brings the increase, the growth. Whatever it is to look like. It's God's work.

THE PROCESS

The actions of missional congregations are provoked, not dictated. The process of renewal is an art form. It is slower. It takes time. It requires patience. A church will first change its behavior, and then it will change its thinking. McKnight notes, "Let's remember how cultures are formed: Leaders form and tell a preliminary narrative, act out or model values for others to see and emulate, teach the important principles of faith and practice, and articulate policies that reinforce the values of the organization. These narratives, actions, principles, and policies are then retold, reenacted, retaught, and re-formed by the congregation."[17]

Here is how I understand the process of this change, which will be developed in more detail below.

1. Enabling a new mood within a congregation
2. Creating spaces for contextually attuned theological discernment
3. Engaging three key catalysts
4. Living out embedded practices within the community

The process begins as a congregation develops a mood of trust emerging from the christoformed attitude of its leaders. Three catalysts are introduced into the congregation that changes its actions and focus: (1) New practices are encouraged within the congregation. These bottom-up practices, over time, begin to change the very character of the congregation. (2) New spaces of discernment are created so that the congregation can hear from each other and the Lord. (3) And then new ways of being a local congregation arise.

This emerges out of the theologically reflective work in the local congregation. As the people of God, an ecclesial identity is formed, created by attention to word and sacraments. As the temple of the Spirit, a local

17. McKnight and Barringer, *Church Called Tov*, 107.

congregation discerns its missiological context. This is where the congregation is located. This is where it has been rooted and planted. Then, as the body of Christ, the local congregation develops new ecclesial practices, unique to that congregation and mindful of the congregation's history, tradition, and denominational ethos. This theological-missional reflection is undergirded, provoked, and strengthened by habits and practices.

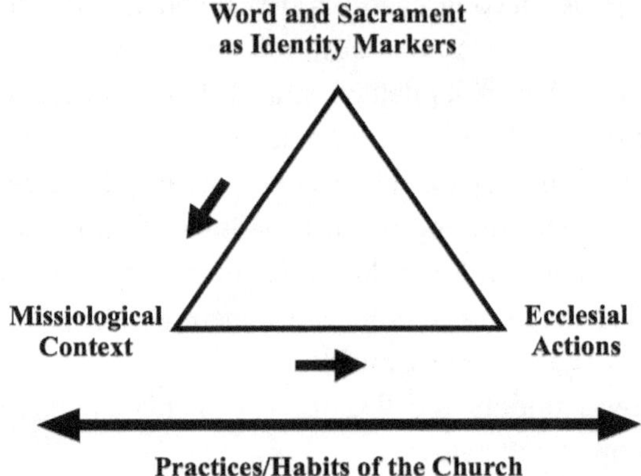

1. Enabling a New Mood Within a Congregation

A congregation that fosters a sense of goodness is a crucial factor for an emerging sense of mission. A congregation's mood will be characterized by the Beatitudes (Matt 5) and the fruit of the Spirit (Gal 5). One can sense this Christlike culture in a congregation. Scot McKnight uses the Hebrew word *tov* to describe this culture: "A Spirit-formed, Christlike culture . . . nurtures truth, offers healing for the wounded, seeks opportunities to show redemptive grace and love, focuses on serving others (rather than on being served), and looks for ways to establish justice in the daily paths of life. A Christlike church culture always has its eyes on people because the mission of the church is all about God's redemptive love for people."[18]

A mood of goodness, developing from a sense of Christoformity, has the promise of transforming a congregation. Cultivating the good soil of a congregation is necessary in order for something new to emerge. JR

18. McKnight and Barringer, *Church Called Tov*, 23.

Woodward, based on the fivefold gifting in Eph 4, paints a picture of what a congregation could look like. He speaks of five environments—learning, healing, welcoming, liberating, and thriving—that can emerge within a healthy congregation.[19]

McKnight further describes such a congregation: "A *tov* church is one where God's goodness permeates the institution, empowering its members—by God's grace—to become people shaped by God's design, which is Christlikeness (or Christoformity). *Tov* people, Christlike people, are characterized by empathy, grace, putting other people first, truth telling, justice, and service."[20] He continues,

> Compassion will characterize a church's culture when the congregation and leaders consistently interact in compassionate ways, until a critical mass of compassion tips the balance in the direction of becoming a compassionate culture. When a church's culture is rooted in compassion, it creates an environment of safety, security, and openness.[21]

This culture of goodness, of Christ-likeness, is a space that nurtures empathy and grace. It puts people first. The congregation is committed to telling the truth and nurturing justice and service.[22] These descriptors give a sense of the culture and environment necessary for good work to happen within a congregation.

Ministry leaders play a key role in the development of this culture. They must be attentive to the culture of a congregation creating an atmosphere where something new might emerge. Pastors of established congregations must remember that a local church existed before they came and will continue after they leave. Pastors hold the church as a steward, with patience and kindness. A local congregation is bigger than any vision and hopes of ministry leaders. Every congregation has a history, traditions, memories, and stories. Pastors must be careful with the church.

As mentioned previously, the call on the lives of ministry leaders in a local setting is to create this atmosphere of *tov*. McKnight writes,

> The pastor is called to nurture a culture of Christoformity . . . we are called to be conformed to Christ. Pastors are nurturers

19. Woodward, *Creating a Missional Culture*, 53.
20. McKnight and Barringer, *Pivot*, 5.
21. McKnight and Barringer, *Church Called Tov*, 16.
22. McKnight and Barringer, *Pivot*, 31.

> of Christoformity in this sense: we are formed by his life, by his death, and by his resurrection and ascension. We are not only to believe the gospel but also to embody it. . . . We become Christoform through participation in Christ: through baptism, through faith, through indwelling and being indwelled by Christ, through the Spirit, through being clothed with Christ, through fellowship, through transformation, and through sharing all the events in Christ's life.[23]

The renewing of a congregation is the Lord's work before it is ours. The Lord is with us in the process. Congregational leaders need to exhibit qualities of patience and humility for the days ahead. New movements do not happen overnight. While we are anxious or frustrated by a lack of progress, the renewal of a congregation requires patience and an atmosphere of trust. This environment is nurtured over time. This is garden work, not machine work. It takes time.

Creating this mood begins with the ministry leaders. At root, it is a matter of heart. When ministry leaders encourage a new attitude, a new stance infects the entire congregation. Scot McKnight and Laura Barringer write,

> Pastors and other leaders exercise a preliminary voice in forming and telling the church's narrative, acting out the Christian life for others to see, teaching the Christian faith and how it is lived, and articulating policies. They exercise formal authority and power to create and maintain the church's culture. Ideally, they do this in a good way. The congregation, both individually and collectively, embraces the culture but also begins to reshape the narrative, act out the Christian life for others to see, reteach the Christian faith, and rearticulate the policies. Thus, the congregation exercises its own authority and power to shape and maintain the culture. Over time, it is the interaction of the leaders and congregation, the congregation and leaders, that forms the culture of a church. In that sense, everyone in the church is "complicit" in whatever culture is formed, good or bad.[24]

Pastoral leaders who demonstrate the characteristics of a gardener, a shepherd, and a servant alter the culture of a congregation. This requires a

23. McKnight, *Pastor Paul*, 4.

24. McKnight and Barringer, *Church Called Tov*, 15. They quote Dietrich Bonhoeffer, who said "the church's word gains weight and power not through concepts but by example" (McKnight and Barringer, *Pivot*, 91).

demonstration of the ways of humility and servanthood. Sondra Wheeler writes, "Because ministers will continually be preaching by behavior and teaching by example, they must also become certain kinds of people: not only people who possess certain knowledge and techniques but also people whose character is shaped in particular ways."[25]

Christoformity is lived. It demonstrates the fruit of the Spirit. It is the way of the cross. These are character qualities. They are necessary first ingredients. Paul says, "Follow my example, as I follow the example of Christ" (1 Cor 11:1). This is what ministry leaders aspire toward. Paul writes,

> For the appeal we make does not spring from error or impure motives, nor are we trying to trick you. On the contrary, we speak as those approved by God to be entrusted with the gospel. We are not trying to please people but God, who tests our hearts. You know we never used flattery, nor did we put on a mask to cover up greed—God is our witness. We were not looking for praise from people, not from you or anyone else, even though as apostles of Christ we could have asserted our authority. (1 Thess 2:3–6)

Modeling the way emerges out of the leader's personal life. It begins with a desire to be a committed follower of Jesus. Leaders abide in Christ. They practice disciplines that develop their personal walk with the Lord. They demonstrate an ongoing discipleship.

This is lived out through ministry leaders being attentive to their emotional health. As Pete Scazzero notes, emotionally healthy leaders face their shadow side, lead out of their marriage/singleness, slow down for a loving union, and practice a Sabbath rhythm.[26]

This mood of goodness begins with listening. We need to slow down and listen. Professor Scott Cormode writes,

> Leadership begins with listening. The greatest act of leadership began with the greatest act of listening, when the Word became flesh and dwelt among us. He did not just walk in our shoes; he walked with our feet. Every time God entrusts a person to my care I have to begin by listening, because before I can invite a person into a new story I have to understand that person's particular backstory. I have to understand what matters most to them—what stories define them. Only then will I be able to invite

25. Wheeler, *Minister as Moral Theologian*, loc. 87 of 2608.

26. Scazzero, *Emotionally Healthy Leader*, pt. 1.

> them into a gospel story that gives them hope. Otherwise, I am just treating them as a stereotype.[27]

Pastors need to listen to the Lord and to each other as we struggle into the future. Pastors love and respect their people enough to slow down and listen. This requires patience. Ministry, the life of a congregation, is more like the work of a glacier than an avalanche. This slow work brings about something of beauty. An avalanche, though bringing about change quickly, can be very destructive.

Personal emotional awareness and listening to others leads to a sense of trust. Trust is developed over time. It emerges from the way leaders live their lives. Strong leadership is not based on position or even results, but rather on who a leader is. Bolsinger notes that people will not follow you off the map if they don't trust you on the map.[28]

And of course, ministry leaders need to love and care for their people. The people are more important than any agenda. Church is not a trophy. It is a wonderful and messy group of people. Pastors must have the congregation's best interests at heart. Pastors want them to grow. Pastors want them to live into mission. But first pastors love them! Bonhoeffer writes something very difficult in *Life Together*: "A pastor should never complain about his congregation, certainly never to other people, but also not to God. A congregation has not been entrusted to him in order that he should become its accuser before God and men."[29] Pastors love their people. They love the place where they are serving. This reciprocal love—love the congregation and be loved—is essential to the missional work.

Out of this sense of trust, and listening and care, ministry leaders are able to engage in a process of provoking change. A congregation moving to a missional stance is difficult. The old ways will cease to exist or will be modified greatly. This change is not just a technical change—fixing a problem like a flat tire. Rather, this type of change is adaptive change. Adaptive change is painful. It costs someone something to respond to an adaptive challenge.[30]

This causes anxiety, sadness, and a sense of loss. Ronald Heifetz writes, "People don't resist change. They resist loss. People are not afraid of change.

27. Cormode, *Innovative Church*, 9.
28. Bolsinger, *Canoeing the Mountains*, 14.
29. Bonhoeffer, *Life Together*, 37.
30. Cormode, *Innovative Church*, 181.

They are only afraid of changes that will cost them something."[31] Church leaders must note and pay attention to the emotional responses to change. There is grieving and there is heat. There will even be sabotage and anger. Throughout the process of something new emerging, ministry leaders must attend to those in the congregation, especially those who have been a part of the fellowship for some time.

Congregations are a system. It is wise for ministry leaders to understand systems theory to better understand what is going on in a congregation.[32] Church leaders must care for their people in the midst of the transition. Ministry leaders need to develop the skills of moving people through an adaptive change process. Being missional doesn't mean you stop being pastoral.[33] Shepherding, guiding, and nurturing a local congregation should not be entered into lightly. Pastors can help to move an organization toward wholeness and health, or they can stifle the work.

In this whole process, it is important to say thank-you. A simple thank-you can have enormous impact on another person. Celebrate what is happening in the church. The ways of the future church cannot be dictated, only encouraged. Watch what the Lord does.

2. Creating Spaces for Contextually Attuned Theological Discernment

Change is never easy, but we are compelled to move forward. Gospel urgency demands this. David Bosch writes, "The church is always in a state of crisis and its greatest shortcoming is that it is only occasionally aware of it."[34] Each church must ask the question: Why are we here? In other words, what is our gospel purpose here, in this place, today? The answer to that question drives the mission. This question, and its response, keeps each congregation fresh, alive, and moving forward in its mission.

The transition to a more organic missional church existence cannot be planned. Instead, current systems can only be disturbed and fertile

31. Quoted in Cormode, *Innovative Church*, 182.

32. See Creech, *Family Systems*; Harrington et al., *Leader's Journey*.

33. For more on the concept of adaptive change, see Bolsinger, *Canoeing the Mountains*; Cormode, *Innovative Church*. For a good summary of adaptive change, see Hayden, *Remissioning Church*, ch. 8.

34. Bosch, *Transforming Mission*, 49.

environments nurtured. Building off of Roxburgh's work on missional change, these stages of change will occur in an organization:

- Stage 1—Stability and equilibrium. This is business as usual.
- Stage 2—Discontinuity. There is a growing sense of dis-ease.
- Stage 3—Disembedding. There is a sense that something new might emerge.
- Stage 4—Transition. A change begins to take place.
- Stage 5—Reformation. A new culture is emerging.[35]

This does not happen in a linear fashion. Nor can it be prescribed. Rather, these stages are discerned usually by looking back. As a congregation reflects upon its journey, it is then able to see the Lord's hand at work among the body of Christ. It is gardening. It is cyclical and seasonal.

As a new mood is being developed, a congregation creates spaces for the church to discern who they are and what they are becoming. Cormode writes, "A holding environment is a psychological space uncomfortable enough that a person cannot avoid the problem but safe enough that the person can experiment with a new way of being. We earlier said that you cannot pursue technical means to adaptive ends. Now we know what you should do. Every approach to adaptive change must include creating a holding environment."[36]

We create holding spaces where discernment and listening and vision sharing can take place. This process is organic, provoked not dictated. It is slowing down to discern and imagine. A congregation needs to create opportunities to hear from the Lord and from each other. This is a slow process. It moves at the speed of a garden. As a congregation meets, new insights emerge from a number of points of provocation.

In these holding spaces, a congregation continues to discern who they are. This is the theologically reflective work of the church. It begins with a recognition and a continuing reaffirmation of the congregation's ecclesial identity. This is developed by deep theological convictions centered in word and sacraments. This is the primary place where a congregation's identity is formed. It continues through hearing stories in the congregation and by observing what is happening in the neighborhood. Our theological and ethical understanding of the congregation enhances and limits our ecclesial

35. Roxburgh, *Sky Is Falling*, 54.

36. Cormode, *Innovative Church*, 189.

practices. This is the process that continues to loop as a congregation continues to discern its identity and context and practices:

Theological identity → Ministry context → Ecclesial practices

The mission begins with attention to our Christology and our ecclesiology, manifested in word and sacraments. This reminds a congregation who they are as the people of God, the body of Christ, and the temple of the Spirit. The particular ecclesial identity is further developed through a recognition of a congregation's history, its location in a neighborhood, denominational distinctives, and the history of the congregation and its ecclesial distinctives. This is an ongoing process within a congregation. The distinctives of the location of the congregation are discerned.

From that identity and missional context, new ecclesial practices emerge. The actions of the church will be unique to every congregation because of a theological identity and a local identity in its particular context. There are no easy ways forward. There are no quick steps. Every church is unique.

For a period of time when I was pastor, the leadership team of the church (lay leaders) and the pastoral staff met together once a month in a room at the church. There was no set agenda. We lit a candle representing Christ's presence with us, and then we sat, for about an hour each time. As we sat, someone would pray, read a portion of Scripture, share something on one's heart, or lead out with a hymn or a chorus. We were seeking to create a space where we could hear from the Lord and from each other.

Our leadership team meetings (board meetings) began with a time of Scripture reflection. We wanted to center ourselves in seeking the Lord as we did the business of the church, and we wanted to hear from the Lord and each other as we did that work. Every month, the volunteers of the church would gather for a time of worship, of Scripture reflection, of training, and then break into small groups around our ministry areas. Again, it was a space to hear from the Lord.

Congregations listen to the Lord through Scripture and to each other. As a congregation gathers around the word through sermons, Bible studies, and personal devotions, the Spirit works and disrupts and calls a congregation forward. Church leaders play a key role in encouraging this disruption. Congregations need to share stories about what is happening in their fellowship. Alan Roxburgh writes,

> Great conversations can begin around questions like: "Can you share a story about the first time you came to this congregation?" "Do you remember first moving into your neighborhood? What was it like?" "What have been some of the most life-giving experiences for you in this church?" "When have you most experienced the presence of God in this congregation?" In regular meetings or groups, you can experiment by posing a simple question each time you come together, such as, "Where might you have seen God at work this week?"[37]

The purpose/vision of the congregation is lifted up through sermons, congregational gatherings. It is a slow process of discerning, listening, reflecting. All are involved in the process, living out the priesthood of all believers. Voices from the center and the margins are heard. What is the Lord saying to us? How do we share the good news in this particular place? It is always a fresh word, but a nurtured and reflected word.

A congregation might develop the practice of dwelling in the word. Reading a passage of Scripture over time allows the Lord to speak to a congregation through each other. Alan Roxburgh writes, "It's a way of letting God address us through Scripture, rather than using Scripture only as a tool for imparting new information or confirming existing beliefs. Dwelling in the word invites the Holy Spirit to enliven a biblical text among us, so that we become aware of and responsive to what God is doing. This is a practice of listening to God through the text and through one another."[38]

As a neighborhood changes, or as a congregation develops new eyes for its community, questions are raised. What are the hurts, the aches, the needs here? The church asks in new ways, why are we here? What is our response? How do we do gospel here? Alan Roxburgh writes about listening to our neighbors: "God is abundantly and creatively present in our neighborhoods. What we want to do as God's people is practice how to listen in on what God is up to in the neighborhood so we can join God there. If you are seeking to travel lightly with Jesus, begin by practicing the art of listening to the neighborhood."[39]

Part of this theological reflection is to attend to matters of race, gender, and class. What are the issues confronting a congregation? What are the hurts, the aches, the pain? When gospel light is shed on a situation,

37. Roxburgh, *Joining God, Remaking Church*, 89. See Branson, *Memories, Hopes, and Conversations*.

38. Roxburgh, *Joining God, Remaking Church*, 60.

39. Roxburgh, *Joining God, Remaking Church*, 93.

what new commitments emerge? A congregation's reflection on its identity in light of Scripture causes the congregation to make new affirmations and commitments. A congregation continues to ask, why are we in this place at this time? The realizations of something new come from many place—ministry leaders at the center but also, and maybe most provocatively, from the margins. We hear not just from those with pastoral gifts but also those with apostolic, prophetic, and evangelistic yearnings and aches. And this will be disturbing at times. Ken Wytsma notes,

> We don't want anything or anyone disrupting or subverting the religious climate that allows us to get along by not talking about things we find challenging or that confront our value system. If we did, those in economic, political, or religious power would suddenly feel like their control was slipping away. But by avoiding these difficult and uncomfortable issues, we reinforce privilege.[40]

Emerging out of a theological understanding of the local congregation, there must be an attentiveness to the congregation's context—its neighborhood. What is happening in your neighborhood? What are the needs of those in the neighborhood? What are the social and justice issues that must be addressed? How can your church respond to the cries and the hurts? Knowing who a congregation is and where that congregation is situated, the church can then begin to develop or strengthen ecclesial missional practices within the congregation and in the neighborhood.[41]

3. Engaging Three Key Catalysts

Three major shifts in a congregation push the church in new directions. These catalysts fundamentally shift the mindset and work of a congregation, nudging it toward a more missional stance within the congregation and in the neighborhood.

40. Wytsma, *Myth of Equality*, 94–95. See also Jennings, *Christian Imagination*; Sechrest et al., *Can "White" People Be Saved?*

41. See Roxburgh, *Joining God, Remaking Church*, 102; Hayden, *Remissioning Church*, 58–61. See also Edwards, "Lectio Vicinitas."

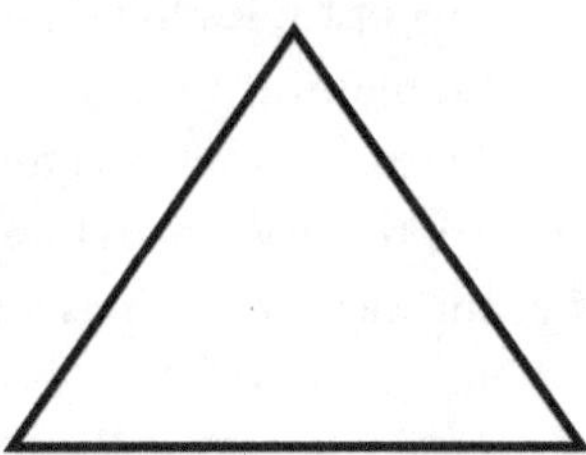

Catalyst 1: Because the church is the people of God, the clergy class must be de-professionalized, while the church retains the value of leaders who serve as interpreters, the catalysts for expositing the word in all its power.[42]

Professional clergy are the greatest impediment to the work of the church. A hierarchical stance of clergy—their roles and titles and positions on the organization chart—not only harms the congregation but creates a bottleneck so that ministry is controlled and implemented by a small group of people. This keeps the congregation at large from seeing and using their gifts and limits the scope of ministry to the narrow giftedness and aspirations of the clergy class. When ministry is given away to the entire church, when pastors let go of their need to control or be admired, whole new vistas of ministry emerge.

While we don't want to give too much power to the clergy, we must recognize that pastors hold great sway, which can hold a congregation captive. Pastors must be willing to move in new directions. The job description of the modern pastor will radically change from professional technician, therapist, or manager to that of missionary, spending significant time with local culture.[43] To again reference Callahan's prophetic words: "The day of the professional minister is over. The day of the missionary pastor has come. . . . The day of the churched culture is over. The day of the mission field has come."[44]

42. Guder, "Walking Worthily," 278.

43. Roxburgh, "Missional Leadership," 196–98.

44. Callahan, *Effective Church Leadership*, 3, 13.

Alan Roxburgh reminds us that the Spirit of God is among people of God, not just the pastor. The single greatest obstacle to mobilizing a congregation is the pastor. Pastors—because of lack of trust, inability to mobilize, or ego needs—can bottleneck a congregation. Nothing changes in a church unless that pastor is able to develop a new vision or the pastor is removed. Roxburgh helps us to imagine how clergy can develop a new understanding of their role in a congregational setting. This creates a different mood and sense of ministry. He notes that God is ahead of us in our neighborhood, calling us to join; God is present in the people who comprise our congregations, and the Spirit is present in their lives and actively inviting them on this journey.[45] God's ordinary people can listen to and hear God through one another as they dwell in the word of God. This changes the role of ministry leaders. Leaders cultivate spaces for listening to the Spirit in life together. A primary work of the ordained is cultivating a people of prayer, who collectively discern the Spirit in the vocation of prayer. The leader must lay down the anxious need to fix the church and make it work again. An ordained leader cannot lead without doing what the baptized are called to do.[46]

Clergy need to develop a new job description and a new stance in the congregation. This is different from the old paradigm of church work. The pastoral leader changes focus. This will disrupt the system more than anything else. This change, decentralizing clergy in a local congregation, is the most significant shift that will bring the most impacting results. This surrendering of power and control by clergy enables an apostolic imagination to permeate the pastoral vocation and will be evident in daily tasks of pastoral leaders.[47]

Pastors, along with other ministry leaders, will be the catalysts for ongoing missional engagement for each person associated with a local congregation. As Professor Kyle Small writes, "Pastoral identity must change: the pastor must not stay primarily into the sanctuary, but she or he must also focus on and animate the same horizon the congregation has in view—outward toward the world."[48] Bonhoeffer suggests that when the church moves into the public square, more clergy will have vocations

45. Roxburgh, *Joining God, Remaking Church*, 54–57.

46. Roxburgh, *Joining God, Remaking Church*, 75.

47. Woodward, *Scandal of Leadership*.

48. Small, "Missional Ordered Ministry," 230.

in the marketplace.[49] This will promote the missional nature of the pastorate, and this will significantly disrupt the current clergy system. Alan Roxburgh writes,

> The classic skills of pastoral leadership in which most pastors were trained were not wrong, but the level of discontinuous change renders many of them insufficient and often unhelpful at this point. . . . The situation requires cultivation of new leadership capacities. Alongside the standard skills of pastoral ministry, leaders need resources and tools to help them cultivate an environment for missional transformation.[50]

This is not an easy shift. Pastors' egos, and even their sense of worth, are on the line. When pastors feel that their professional status and advanced degrees give them a position over others, ministry gets relegated to a few. But a christoform stance begins to break down this attitude. Ministry is given away, ministries expand. Mistakes will be tolerated along the way! We move at the speed, and even the uncertainty, of a garden.

Lessening the power of the clergy class opens the congregation up to a polycentric view of pastoral leadership.[51] Power is not held by a small group represented by a senior pastor but rather by a team of pastors and lay leaders who work in a spirit of cooperation and discernment. This changes the environment of staff meetings, board meetings, and congregational meetings. This moves a congregation beyond a strategic, get-it-done sense, to a more organic flow. A garden.

49. Bonhoeffer writes, "The church is only the church when it exists for others. To make a start, it should give away all its property to those in need. The clergy must live solely on the free-will offerings of their congregations, or possibly engage in some secular calling. The church must share in the secular problems of ordinary human life, not dominating, but helping and serving. It must tell men of every calling what it means to live in Christ, to exist for others" (*Letters and Papers*, 282).

50. Roxburgh and Romanuk, *Missional Leader*, loc. 455 of 4108.

51. See Handley, *Polycentric Mission Leadership*; Brisco, "Co-Vocational Church Planters."

Catalyst 2: Because the church is the body of Christ, the church missionally engages in the world through resisting institutionalization and church conformity. The church develops new structures.

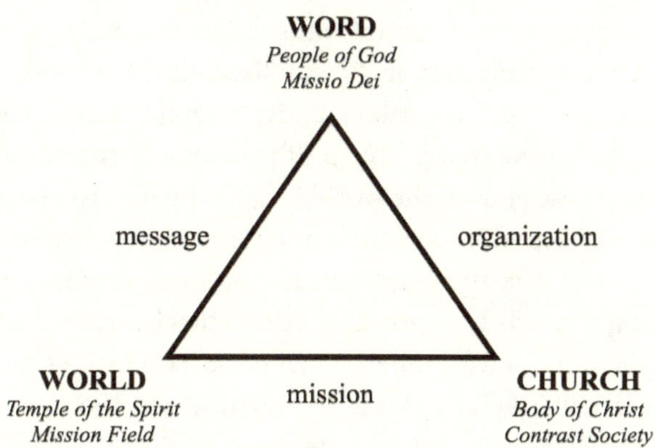

This chart helps us understand the missional nature of a local congregation.[52] The message of the gospel found in Scripture is communicated based on context to particular hearers. The gospel is proclaimed in a way that it can be heard and understood. The mission is dictated by the needs of the world. The organizing structure of a local congregation organization is built on an understanding of the gospel and the uniqueness of a local congregation and its unique history, traditions, and denominational ethos. The local church develops a new polity based on its theological-missional identity. Laypeople are affirmed along with pastoral leaders. Ministry opportunities are expanded. The fivefold gifts in Ephesians are encouraged, developed, and deployed. The implementation of new ecclesial structures moves the church away from centralized, regulatory practices and instead develops new missional polities for innovative mobilization.

Churches need structure, but the best ways to structure a congregation take into account both the institutional and movement aspects of a church. A congregation needs to consider how to be flexible and fluid in the process. How might a congregation move beyond hierarchy, noted for command and control, and bottlenecks, and seek a more flattened structure?

52. This chart builds off the work of Lesslie Newbigin. See Hunsberger, "Newbigin Gauntlet," 9; Franke, *Missional Theology*, 64.

Notice the difference between a starfish and a spider.[53] This is like two different models for a church. Spiders and starfish look similar. They both have central bodies with legs that sprout radially from the center. But there are big differences between these two organisms. If you cut off the head of a spider, you kill the entire organism. Spider organizations, by extension, are standard hierarchies where a central brain or decision-making body regulates the actions of the organization in a centralized, direct fashion. If something bad happens to that decision-making body, the entire organization dies.

Starfish don't have that problem. If you cut a starfish in half and fling each half to opposite ends of the world, what happens? You get two starfish. A starfish has in each of its cells all that it needs to regenerate a whole new starfish. Every cell of a starfish organization, unlike spider organizations, has everything it needs to reproduce. Alan Hirsch writes, "The metaphor of the spider and the starfish offers us an important insight into the nature of what we can call 'fragile systems' of organization. The more one focuses intelligence and power in the few, the more fragile is that system. This is different from 'antifragile' systems, where power and function are dispersed as widely as possible. When the church is viewed through the lenses of fragility and antifragility, it's quite simple to discern the primary form that the New Testament church took."[54] How can congregations develop systems that are more characteristic of a starfish rather than a spider? Moving in new directions creates a different mood in a congregation and opens up the possibilities of more missional engagement by those who are a part of that congregation. You don't need a title to serve. You don't need to be elected to a board. You don't need to develop a prospectus that is approved by a governing body. A starfish congregation is able to move organically, based on the gift mix of people in the church, to do ministry in the congregation and in the neighborhood.

This becomes a bit more difficult for congregations within a denomination or with an established history, denominational or independent. Still, beginning to explore ways to simplify and broaden structures within a congregation will lead toward freeing a congregation up for more extensive ministry, making a congregation nimbler.

A conversation about a change in structure or polity will be difficult in some contexts. A both/and, rather than an either/or, direction could

53. This metaphor is developed in Ford et al., *Starfish and the Spirit*; Brafman and Beckstrom, *Starfish and the Spider*.

54. As quoted in Ford et al., *Starfish and the Spirit*, 2–3.

be helpful. A local congregation that has a formal, and perhaps strict, structure—a spider organization—can think about ways to still embody elements of starfish thinking. The purpose of such an exercise is to free the congregation up for increased missional activity and encourage innovation. This innovation can take the form of experiments or projects.[55] These would be short-term projects with time limits. At the end of that period, the project is evaluated and next steps are determined. The project could be concluded or it could keep going. This is not remaking the congregation. It is simply giving freedom for something new to emerge.

How might structures working within denominational constraints be changed so that ministry might be more innovative and nimbler? Traditional polities are important. They become points of check and balance, even brakes, that keep a congregation from bad decisions and consequences. But they can also be used to stifle innovation and creativity. Faithful congregations must hold to structures and procedures that protect the church and people within the church. But those procedures must not be allowed to keep the congregation from moving in new directions.

Churches can so easily get caught up in the busyness of the business of church that ministry is thwarted. Churches can worry so much about policies and procedures that the very life of the church is squelched. Churches can be so afraid of making a mistake that the church never moves. We need to ease up. Accept imperfection. Let experiences become opportunities for learning. Be careful, wise, and prudent, but risk. Rather than making every church decision a matter of vote, churches can try experimenting with new ideas. These pilot projects may succeed or not. In experiments, failure is not bad; it is just a learning opportunity. It is risky to give up control, but moving beyond a command-and-control attitude and structure allows for innovation.

Sometimes structures limit opportunities for ministry. Bob was an elected deacon in our congregation. For a time, we had an official deacon board that met monthly to discuss all matters of business. After Bob had served one term on the board and was up for reelection, he came to me and said, "Pastor, I just want to care for people. I don't want to be stuck in a business meeting." Bob did not go back on the deacon board, but rather spent his time following his gifts and heart's desire—he cared for people.

55. See Bolsinger and Watson's conversation on small experiments: "Learning Our Way Forward."

Catalyst 3: Because the church is the temple of the Holy Spirit, the church reimagines its work in the world and in the church. The Spirit is on the move. God is ahead of us. God is at work at the center and at the margins. Our scorecards for faithfulness and fruitfulness change.

Most churches base their success or vitality on measures such as baptisms, membership budgets, attendance, number of paid staff, and buildings. These measurements follow a standard mindset in the business world. In the past, the legitimacy of a church has been based on a physical building, a respected pastor, a growing membership, significant attendance at weekend worship, and being part of a denomination.[56] A church's striving to succeed and the pastor's ambition to be known can keep a church measuring success by bodies, baptisms, buildings, and budgets. Lesslie Newbigin reminds us, "We do not find Paul concerning himself with the size of churches or with questions about their growth. His primary concern is with their faithfulness, with the integrity of their witness."[57] When we think more like a garden than a machine, the mood of a sent congregation changes. Van Gelder offers a perspective on how priorities shift in the mission of the church:

- From maintenance to mission
- From membership to discipleship
- From pastor centered to lay empowered
- From chaplaincy for self to hospitality for others
- From focus on ourselves to focus on the world
- From settled to sent[58]

Determining success on the basis of bodies, budgets, baptisms is machinelike thinking. Vitality is expressed as bigger, better, and larger. But if we look at congregations more as a garden, our measurements change. A garden's vitality is measured differently. Sometimes a garden is thriving. In other seasons, a garden is dormant. There are a number of factors that impact the garden. We need to evaluate and assess, but we must move beyond machinelike thinking.

56. See Packard, "Organizational Structure, Religious Belief," 111.

57. Newbigin, *Open Secret*, 125.

58. Van Gelder, *Essence of the Church*, 37–38. See also works such as Van Gelder, *Ministry of Missional Church*; Van Gelder and Zscheile, *Missional Church in Perspective.*

The future is going to look different from the past. Van Engen notes that numerical growth is not the measure of a church, but rather the church's yearning for growth as an instrument of God's mission in the world. We must resist the exaltation of numbers and of technique.[59]

Reggie McNeal calls local churches to develop new scorecards that indicate the how fruitful and faithful a congregation is. This requires a move from internal indicators to external indicators. There is a shift in priority from programs to people. A new mindset is developed that stresses kingdom-based, expansive leadership over contained and limited church-based leadership.[60] A healthy congregation is able to live out its mission within the fellowship and in the neighborhood. Every congregation needs to develop its own new metrics through tending and nurturing, rather than action steps.[61]

The church can be more like a garden than a machine. These three catalysts related to clergy, structure, and measurement disrupt the normalized procedures of a congregation. This is the work of provoking the system, the garden. It gives congregation new lenses to assess its life and its functions. These catalysts alter the mood and functions of a congregation, leading to new missional vitality, both internally and externally.

4. Living Out Embedded Practices Within the Community

Newbigin sees the local congregation as the dominant location for which "the reality of the new creation is present, known, and experienced, and primarily for the sake of mission."[62] This is where the work gets done: in very ordinary, routine, and local churches. Followers of Jesus in every congregation are in the process of being formed into the image of Christ (Gal 4:19). This is what McKnight calls Christoformity.[63] We are called to become like Christ in every aspect of our lives, including our lives together in our congregation. This is a life conforming to Christ, striving for unity and peace as sisters and brothers in Christ.

59. Charles Van Engen, *The Growth of the True Church*; as cited in Paas, *Church Planting in West*, 121, 250.

60. McNeal, *Kingdom Come*; *Missional Renaissance*.

61. For some possible new measurements, see Evangelical Covenant Church, "pH Check." See also Vaters, *De-Sizing the Church*, 180; Yang et al., *Becoming a Future-Ready Church*.

62. Sunquist and Yong, *Gospel and Pluralism Today*, 111.

63. McKnight, *Pastor Paul*, 4.

Our behaviors, our practices, change our attitudes. New practices give us new insights into ourselves and the world around us. Practices are simple steps engaged over time. This begins to change our life. Scot McKnight and Laura Barringer write,

> Let's try to understand how a culture forms into an active agent. The theory works like this: Practices and acts form into habits. Habits form into a culture agent (a group taking on the power to influence). The culture agent acts upon humans to conform to the culture. We practice habits that deepen the culture. And around and around we go in the same direction. This all means that the congregation is an agent of culture influence, formation, and transformation. If the culture brims with toxins, such as having a desire for fame, glory, and money, the congregation will distort people away from Christlikeness. If the culture is *tov*, the congregation will shape toward *tov*.[64]

Benjamin Conner adds, "Christian practices are the embodied signs, instruments, and foretastes of the kingdom of God that Christian people participate in together over time to partake in, partner with, and witness to God's redemptive presence for the life of the world in Jesus Christ."[65]

Because this new way of being the church is more provoked than dictated, practices are introduced into a local congregation that become tangible, practical ways to live out a faithful life. These practices, over time, instill a new way of being the church in the routines of life and ministry.

I started playing guitar again after many years of letting it lie dormant. In order to get better, I need to practice. I am not a great guitar player. I have no ambition to play in front of anyone except my grandkids, but I want to be good. Learning something new on my guitar—a lick, a technique, a chord transition—takes time. (My pinky finger has a mind of its own!) But as I practice, I simply show up and work at a new skill, and I do get better. It just takes time. My dentist says I need to floss only the teeth I want to keep. So, every day (almost) I floss. It is a simple activity. It doesn't take much time, but the results are important and good.

So it is with spiritual habits and practices. They are not extraordinary. They are quite mundane but, over time, these habits change the way we think and feel. These practices change a person. Similarly, habits practiced by a congregation, over time, change the mood of a congregation. The

64. McKnight and Barringer, *Pivot*, 157.

65. Conner, *Practicing Witness*, loc. 940–42 of 1680.

congregation's mood shifts. Being more conformed to the image of Christ and growing deeper in unity and care for each other, worship is enriched, and an ache for the good of the neighborhood increases. Richard Rohr writes, "We do not think ourselves into new ways of living. We live ourselves into new ways of thinking."[66]

In ordinary practices, beneath the surface, the Lord is working. We need to learn to pay attention to the subtle workings of the Lord's Spirit. Hayden writes, "Our shared habits as a church give expression and voice to what we hope for, what we lament, and what we ignore. There is an incredible link between the habits (informed by what we called rituals, practices, language, and places in our cultural exegesis charts) and the vision of flourishing and God's rule and reign being fulfilled."[67]

One of the tasks of pastors is to see how each and every situation might be an occasion for seeing transformation. Peterson writes,

> The pervasive element in our two-thousand-year pastoral tradition is not someone who "gets things done" but rather the person placed in the community to pay attention and call attention to "what is going on right now" between men and women, with one another and with God—this kingdom of God that is primarily local, relentlessly personal, and prayerful "without ceasing."[68]

The work is always toward forming. As I stated earlier, the goal for a local congregation is:

> Forming people/a congregation into the image of Christ (discipleship), in the context of the local church (community) on mission (*missio Dei*).

It is always toward Christ, as a community, and never settled but always sent. In practices—worship, personal practices, congregational practices—we mature in our faith, care for each other, and engage in our world.

Worship

Worship is a key factor in the life of a congregation. The people of God gather in worship. In a variety of ways and forms, a congregation gathers to worship. This is the primary practice of the church. Eugene Peterson writes,

66. Rohr, *Everything Belongs*, 20.
67. Hayden, *Remissioning Church*, 88–89.
68. Peterson, *Pastor*, 5.

"The congregational consensus emerged not so much by talking about it but by simply doing it: worship was our signature activity, the distinctive act that set us apart from all other social structures—schools, businesses, athletic teams, political parties, government agencies."[69] The church in worship develops a number of important postures:

- Come—the church gathers.
- Stand—the church stands to offer praise.
- Kneel—the church prays.
- Sit—the church hears the word.
- Eat—the church shares in the Lord Supper.
- Go—the church goes into the world in witness.[70]

A congregation's identity is built around the word, the baptismal font and pool, and the table. God's people must gather to remember who they are and to worship the God who loves them, calls them together, and sends them out in mission. Scott Sunquist says it this way:

> The church, the body of Christ, has two basic purposes for its existence: worship and witness. All other functions point to and should aid in fulfilling these two purposes. . . . As a healthy organism breathes in and breathes out, so the church goes out in mission and returns to receive needed oxygen in community worship. . . . As the church goes out in mission, the church is the presence of Jesus Christ among the nations: loving, healing, including, proclaiming, and reconciling.[71]

Worship and witness. The local congregation gathers in corporate worship. It will take a number of different forms based on the ethos of the particular congregation, but gathering together, as sisters and brothers in Christ, to worship the Lord is the primary action. Missional activity in the congregation and in the neighborhood emerges from this ongoing, regular activity.

The apostle Paul reminds us that our whole lives are to be an act of worship: "Therefore, I urge you, brothers and sisters, in view of God's mercy, to offer your bodies as a living sacrifice, holy and pleasing to God—this is your true and proper worship. Do not conform to the pattern of this world,

69. Peterson, *Pastor*, 172.

70. Adapted from Sunquist, *Why Church?*, loc. 325 of 4540.

71. Sunquist, *Understanding Christian Mission*, 281–82.

but be transformed by the renewing of your mind. Then you will be able to test and approve what God's will is—his good, pleasing and perfect will" (Rom 12:1–2). Therefore, the church corporately and individually engages in additional practices that embody whole-life worship. Followers of Jesus engage in a number of practices: personal and congregational.

Personal Practices

Every follower of Jesus should be encouraged to develop spiritual practices that help a person grow in their faith. These include regular time in the word and prayer, fasting and solitude, serving others, and practicing Sabbath. In all these ways, through these practices, we become more like Jesus. We are shaped into the image of Christ. This impacts not only our lives and our families and our church, but it also becomes a marker in our community.[72]

As a congregation commits to make spiritual habits a part of their life together and as these practices become part of the normal rhythm of life, change occurs. It's like physical exercise; over time, a person can see good results. It doesn't happen overnight, but the results are significant. This changes the mood of people in the congregation. Such practices open the eyes and hearts of a congregation to new missional imaginations.

Congregational Practices

At a congregational level, core commitments are introduced into a church that sets a mood for how a congregation lives out its life. Such practices develop the character of a congregation. As they are encouraged and lived out, they can change the very nature of a local congregation. This happens subtly, even subversively, over time, but it will change a congregation. David Fitch develops seven practices lived out in a congregation that impact a church and lead it toward a greater sense of Christoformity.

1. The practice of the Lord's Table is centered around the presence of Jesus. When we gather with others to participate in this, we tend to God's presence in our lives.

72. For more practices, see Foster, *Celebration of Discipline*; Willard, *Spirit of the Disciplines*. See also a structure for personal practices called BELLS developed by Michael Frost in *Surprise the World*.

2. The practice of reconciliation: In a sin-scarred and divided world, the practice of reconciliation puts us at the heart of the message of God: shalom with God and others.
3. The practice of proclaiming the gospel: The practice of proclamation is announcing—with hope—that this is God's world and he desires for his presence to break in even further.
4. The practice of the fivefold gifting: The fivefold gifting allows us to receive God's gifts poured out to different people who work together to advance God's mission.
5. The practice of being with the least of these: Being with the least of these isn't just a good idea or warm sentiment but the very way in which God makes his presence known among us.
6. The practice of being with children: The practice of being with children shows us the values of the kingdom: wonder, celebration, dependence, honesty, and playfulness.
7. The practice of kingdom prayer: The practice of kingdom prayer is the acknowledgment of our submission to God, our desire to be more accessible for his purposes, and a longing for more of his presence.[73]

As practices like these are encouraged and embedded, a congregation will act differently. The practices will change the way people in the church relate to each other and impact the way the church as a whole, and individuals within, respond to the world for the neighbor's good.

Two key practices are essential in the life of a congregation.[74] Hospitality and the Lord's Table point toward a kingdom reality. These two key overlapping practices impact a congregation and set it up to be a new type of church in mission, within the congregation and beyond. They change how we are church and give a glimpse of what is envisioned in the worldwide diverse kingdom of God.

We cannot remain the same as we live out these practices within a congregation. These congregational practices, encouraged and modeled by the ministry leaders, alter the mood of a congregation for the better. They develop an atmosphere of love, kindness, humility, and transparency. They lead to a deeper sense of trust. They foster a missional movement within the congregation.

73. Fitch, *Faithful Presence*, 23–25.

74. See the appendix for more on these two practices.

This ongoing nurturing of a congregation—through enabling a new mood to develop, creating an environment for reflection, interjecting transforming catalysts, and practicing new habits as a congregation and individually—will lead to new actions and opportunities for ministry within the congregation and in the neighborhood.

A congregation changes slowly over time, and it becomes different. When we see the growth, the change, it is all worth it. When we don't see it, we remember that it is the Lord's work. We plant and water, and the Lord brings the increase. Forming people into the image of Christ—this is good work! This becomes our prayer:

> Father, We yearn to be the church you want us to become. Shape us into something beautiful. We recognize that you are the Potter and we are the clay, please continue to mold us into the image of Christ. We want to join in what you are already doing in the world. In our worship and life together, in our ministry and service to others, we want to give people a glimpse of your intentions for the whole world. Help us to welcome the outcasts, love our enemies, and form a community that is visibly different from the culture around us as a sign of what you are doing in the world. Help us experience your love and grace, grow in our relationship with Jesus, and experience the power of your Spirit as we offer your good news to others. In Jesus' name we pray, Amen.[75]

75. Woodward, *Scandal of Leadership*, 295.

5

Heart

Christ's love compels us to nurture missional communities of worship, discipleship, care, and witness. Pastors who have a primary role in advancing missional communities must attend to matters of their own heart. They do this to develop a mood of goodness and health in their lives, and within the congregation, so that they might serve well and so that the congregation will flourish. This is not always easy. Forces internal and external can make this task difficult. Ministry flows from the inside out. Pastor and church consultant Jim Herrington, Trisha Taylor, and R. Robert Creech write,

> Embarking on the journey of personal transformation-apprenticing with Jesus Christ to learn how to live and how to lead-is what it means to be a pastor in the twenty-first century. Personal transformation in one's own life is the only foundation on which effective leadership can be constructed. To the degree that we are personally being transformed, we are able to lead the way as our congregations change, so that they will be available to God for the transformation of their community. We can find God's grace and power through personal change, to know and do the right thing.[1]

Pastors have the ability, the power, to do great good through a community and to its members or to inflict great harm on a community and those who are a part of that community. Pastors must be healthy: physically, mentally, emotionally, relationally, and spiritually. This is an essential

1. Herrington et al., *Leader's Journey*, 25.

matter for ministry leaders to attend to as a local congregation seeks to be a sent community. Lesslie Newbigin writes,

> The minister's leadership of the congregation in its mission to the world will be first and foremost in the area of his or her own discipleship, in that life of prayer and daily consecration which remains hidden from the world but which is the place where the essential battles are either won or lost.[2]

Ministry leaders want to live out their call with excellence and joy. Over time that sense of joy fades. Ministry takes a heavy toll. Pastors are robbed of joy, and that joy is replaced with exhaustion, cynicism, and discouragement. Pastors can serve well only if we begin by taking care of our insides. Pastor Peter Marty, writing a column in *The Christian Century*, notes that demoralization among pastors is high but suggests we need a narrative other than burnout to describe the situation. Marty suggests that "a crisis of spirit" is the larger issue; it is "a loss of meaning. An absence of what Howard Thurman calls 'an aliveness within.'"[3]

Pastors are called into ministry because their hearts are gripped by the Lord. They resonate with Eugene Peterson, who says,

> I've loved being a pastor, almost every minute of it. It's a difficult life because it's a demanding life. But the rewards are enormous—the rewards of being on the front line of seeing the gospel worked out in people's lives. I remain convinced that if you are called to it, being a pastor is the best life there is.[4]

He loved being a pastor, almost every minute of it. Pastors understand. Lillian Daniel expresses the same sense:

> I love being a minister. Even when the ministry is hard, it's more fun than any other job I can imagine. Where else can you preach, teach, meet with a lead abatement specialist, and get arrested for civil disobedience all in the same week? . . . But mostly I love observing God's presence in the lives of people of faith. Mostly I love the moments when, from the position of paying holy attention to my own community of faith, I notice the power and presence of God.[5]

2. Newbigin, *Gospel in Pluralist Society*, 240–41.
3. Marty, "Privilege of Ministry," para. 6.
4. Peterson, "Best Life," para. 6.
5. Daniel, *Odd and Wondrous Calling*, 2.

Pastors know what this is like. Each week, there is another list of mundane tasks to complete, yet, often mixed in with the mundane, there are also moments of clarity and transcendence.

Reggie McNeal said to serve a church with a sense of call is hard; to serve a church without a call is cruel and unusual self-punishment.[6] Pastors face frustration, loneliness, and fatigue. There are moments of doubt. Pastors face missed expectations from others. Pastors experience betrayal and questioning of motives and intrusions into life and family. In those moments, pastors wonder whether it is all worth it. Ministry leaders must take care of themselves for the sake of the ministry, those entrusted to their care, and simply for themselves. This is not new. Look at the experience of the apostle Paul:

> We do not want you to be uninformed, brothers and sisters, about the troubles we experienced in the province of Asia. We were under great pressure, far beyond our ability to endure, so that we despaired of life itself. Indeed, we felt we had received the sentence of death. But this happened that we might not rely on ourselves but on God, who raises the dead. (2 Cor 1:8–9)
>
> Therefore we do not lose heart. Though outwardly we are wasting away, yet inwardly we are being renewed day by day. (2 Cor 4:16)
>
> For when we came into Macedonia, we had no rest, but we were harassed at every turn—conflicts on the outside, fears within. (2 Cor 7:5)

Conflicts on the outside. Unreasonable or unmet expectations put on us or by us. We are met with criticism. Pastors are always on call with demands by people, meetings, and crises. There are money issues. No clear job descriptions. Secondary trauma. Pastors' families suffer from the expectations put on spouses and children. Pastors are people pleasers. Stanley Hauerwas once said pastors are a quivering mass of availability; we seek to please everyone and, in the process, it is like we are being "nibbled to death by ducks."[7]

Fears on the inside. Pastors are subject to burnout, depression, fatigue, obesity, stress, relational troubles, and spiritual dryness. Pastors know how to fake it—say all the right things while dead inside. We are often involved

6. McNeal, *Work of Heart*, 131.

7. As quoted in Willimon, *Pastor*, 72; Willimon and Hauerwas, "Dangers of Pastoral Care," para. 11.

in task switching: going from a wedding to a funeral, the best and the toughest in a matter of moments causing ministerial whiplash. Pastors want ministry to move like an avalanche, but it moves at the speed of a glacier. That causes more self-doubt, let alone the criticism by church people who wonder: Why isn't our church, pastor, like the one down the street? In the words of J. R. Briggs, we are "BLASTED": bored, lonely, angry or anxious, stressed, tired, envious, distracted or depressed.[8]

Pastors get this. This type of experience is not unique to pastors, but pastors do experience this, and it can have devastating consequences for a church and for the pastor's own life and family. Very often pastors suffer alone. Pastors are subject to disappointment, fatigue, frustration, and despair. The joy that once was a hallmark of ministry drains away. A pastor's personal life, family life, and ministry life degrade. Henri Nouwen reached a crisis point in his life:

> As I entered into my fifties and was able to realize the unlikelihood of doubling my years, I came face to face with the simple question, "Did becoming older bring me closer to Jesus?" After twenty-five years of priesthood, I found myself praying poorly, living somewhat isolated from other people, and very much preoccupied with burning issues. Everyone was saying that I was doing really well, but something inside was telling me that my success was putting my own soul in danger. I began to ask myself whether my lack of contemplative prayer, my loneliness, and my constantly changing involvement in what seemed most urgent were signs that the Spirit was gradually being suppressed. It was very hard for me to see clearly, and though I never spoke about hell or only jokingly so, I woke up one day with the realization that I was living in a very dark place and that the term "burnout" was a convenient psychological translation for a spiritual death.[9]

In response, he wrote a book on Christian leadership: *In the Name of Jesus*. He notes that Christian leaders easily fall into three temptations: to be relevant and productive, to be spectacular and win applause, to be powerful (leading, not being led).[10] These temptations seek to overcome the bleakness in a ministry leader's soul, but these fixes don't work. They create more harm for pastors and those entrusted to their care. Arch Hart writes,

8. Briggs, "Are You Blasted?"

9. Nouwen, *In Name of Jesus*, 13.

10. Nouwen, *In Name of Jesus*, 35–37.

"Pastors don't get in trouble because they forget they are pastors. They get in trouble because they forget they are persons."[11]

When I was a pastor, I had a standing monthly check-in call with another pastor. We shared about the joys and struggles in our ministry. We shared about what was going on in our lives. The goal of the meeting was simply to keep each other in ministry for one more month! We took turns being the encourager or the discouraged. Thankfully, we were never the discouraged one in the same month! I had a written-out resignation letter that I kept in my desk drawer. It was a pity letter. I never gave it to anyone. A memory of that letter reminds me how hard the work can be.

Pastor and ministry podcaster Carey Nieuwhof lists a number of things he wished someone had told him before becoming a pastor:

- Your character will be tested more than your competency will be.
- Leading people is more difficult than reading Greek.
- Strategy matters as much as mission and vision.
- You will be tempted to cheat on your family because you love God.
- Mentors aren't optional.
- Just because your organization is growing doesn't mean you should do more.
- Perseverance is underrated.[12]

Though the work is not easy, if called to it, it is the best life there is. So we must care for ourselves. If we don't, we bring harm to ourselves and others. Pastors become too busy caught up in the corporate nature of church. Their ego begins to get the best of them, basking in the flattering comments people make about them. The pastor's attitude becomes one of thinly veiled contempt toward those entrusted to their care. Pastors simply go through the motions; it is mediocrity masquerading as faithfulness.[13] Pastors forget that they are accountable to others and to the Lord, leading to dangerous narcissistic tendencies. As Diane Langberg notes, the mantra of a

11. As quoted in First Coast Churches, "Pastor Wellness Pathway"; Sevier County Baptist Association, "Pastor Wellness."

12. Nieuwhof, "How to Start Ministry."

13. Jones and Armstrong, *Resurrecting Excellence*, loc. 341 of 2425.

narcissistic spiritual leader is "I am bigger, I am better, and I have no interest in understanding my impact on you except in so far as you can feed my ego."[14]

This can happen so easily and subtly. Pastors rarely begin this way, but this way creeps into their ministry and it does great harm. J. R. Briggs writes, "The fine line between healthy and unhealthy pastoral work is found in the motivations of our hearts."[15] Pastors stand in front of others and proclaim the word of God. Pastors have their names on websites and on letterhead. Pastors have titles. Pastors are put on a pedestal. Pastors are professionals with advanced degrees. Pastors have an office that holds them in high esteem. Pastors can become toxic. Willimon writes, "The great ethical danger for clergy is not that we might 'burn out,' . . . not that we might lose the energy required to do ministry. Our danger is that we might 'black out,' that is lose consciousness of why we are here and who we are called to be for Christ and his church. . . . Periodic refurbishment of our vision is needed."[16]

Pastors also are in the process of being formed into the image of Christ (Gal 4:19), Christoformity.[17] We are called to become like Christ in every aspect of our lives, including our lives together in our congregation. This is a life conforming to Christ, striving for unity and peace as sisters and brothers in Christ. This is a mood of humility. Max DePree reminds us, "The first responsibility of a leader is to define reality. The last is to say thank you. In between the two, the leader must become a servant and a debtor."

Ministry flows from the inside out. How do we survive being a pastor? How do we make it work. I am convinced that the only way is to lead from the heart. Peterson notes,

> The congregation is the pastor's place for developing vocational holiness. It goes without saying that it is the place of ministry: we preach the word and administer the sacraments, we give pastoral care and administer community life, we teach and we give spiritual direction. But it is also the place in which we develop virtue, learn to love, advance in hope—become what we preach.[18]

14. DeGroat, *When Narcissism Comes*, 68.
15. Briggs, *Fail*, 68.
16. Willimon, *Calling and Character*, 21.
17. McKnight, *Pastor Paul*, 4.
18. Peterson, *Under the Unpredictable Plant*, 21.

CYCLES OF MINISTRY[19]

The issue of pastoral identity takes on a new perspective as we view our cycling through life. Ministry is never static. With Paul in Phil 3:12, we "press on." Ministry is always fluid and challenging. We ask four questions along the way at different stages in our ministry journey, and we also ask these questions throughout our ministry life.

1. How Might I Serve?

First, we ask, Lord, how might I serve? We sense the call to ministry on our lives. We can't imagine doing anything else. We are excited about ministry. Sometimes we get paid and feel guilty for being paid for something we love to do. For some, the question gets more complicated, especially for women serving in ministry. There are additional questions about getting proper schooling, when to start a family, and how to juggle marriage and work and family. There is a deeper question that we ask not just at the beginning of our ministry life but throughout our life. When we ask, how might I serve, we are also asking, *To whom do I belong?* This deeper question is one of allegiance and commitment. We sacrifice; we surrender; we take up the cross. We do this early on in our ministry, and we do it throughout.

2. What Am I Doing?

Second, after just a few years in ministry we ask, what am I doing? The idealism of ministry fades. Ministry becomes harder. People are hard. The work is hard. We realize that we don't know as much as we thought we did. Many drop out of ministry at around years five to eight. It is not easy. The deeper question that we ask throughout our lives is: *How do I stay faithful and fruitful?* We realize that the tasks of ministry are hard. We cannot do this work in our own strength. So, we commit to abide in Christ (John 15). We can serve well because we trust that the Lord will strengthen us.

19. This initial work, and the first question in each section below, is drawn from my Evangelical Covenant Church friend and colleague Dan Pietryzyk; see Pietryzyk, "Shooting the Rapids." See also the work of Terry Walling at Leader Breakthru; Clinton, *Making of a Leader*.

3. Do I Want to Do This for the Rest of My Life?

Third, a bit later in ministry we ask, do I want to do this for the rest of my life? Mid-career, we get tired. The work is rewarding but exhausting. The rewards don't always outweigh the costs, personally and to one's family. So, we ask the hard question around years thirteen to fifteen about remaining in this work or doing something new. This is another period of walking away from ministry.

I am convinced that lifelong learning is so critical at both of these stages. We need good supportive people around us, a place to vent and to pray. We need to engage our minds with new thinking. We need to develop new skills. We need encouragement to refresh our own walk with the Lord.

Those who make it through enter into a wonderful season of ministry. They are wiser. They are able to discern better between what is important and what is not. They know the difference between fads and gimmicks and those paradigms that are generative and transforming. These can be the very best years of ministry characterized by personal humility and professional will.[20]

The deeper question is: *How do I endure with hope?* Paul faced challenges throughout his ministry. He said, "We were harassed at every turn—conflicts on the outside, fears within" (2 Cor 7:5). Paul was able to endure, and so are we because we take a new stance in life—one of weakness and humility. In Paul's words in 2 Cor 4:1, 7, "Therefore, since through God's mercy we have this ministry, we do not lose heart. . . . But we have this treasure in jars of clay to show that this all-surpassing power is from God and not from us."

4. How Do I Finish Well?

Fourth, later in ministry, if we hang in, we ask, how do I finish well? With greater degrees of wisdom and maturity, we are able to minister to others and mentor. We pour into the lives of others, watching them succeed and flourish, helping them to avoid some of the mistakes we made along the way. This is a period of significant impact. The deeper question is: *How do I build in practices and create community now?* We must order our lives in such a way that we can finish well. At each stage, and our whole life long, we all need to gather with community of support, a commitment to lifelong

20. Collins, *Good to Great.*

learning, and a determination to cultivate our walk with the Lord. Finishing well begins early in our ministry. So, we press on!

Through all these phases, there must be a new stance in life. It is not tall-steeple pride, arrogance, and privilege. It is rather weakness and humility. This is the lesson Paul learned; this is how Paul could keep going!

> Therefore, since through God's mercy we have this ministry, we do not lose heart. . . . But we have this treasure in jars of clay to show that this all-surpassing power is from God and not from us. We are hard pressed on every side, but not crushed; perplexed, but not in despair; persecuted, but not abandoned; struck down, but not destroyed. We always carry around in our body the death of Jesus, so that the life of Jesus may also be revealed in our body. For we who are alive are always being given over to death for Jesus' sake, so that his life may also be revealed in our mortal body. So then, death is at work in us, but life is at work in you. (2 Cor 4:1, 7–12)
>
> Therefore, in order to keep me from becoming conceited, I was given a thorn in my flesh, a messenger of Satan, to torment me. Three times I pleaded with the Lord to take it away from me. But he said to me, "My grace is sufficient for you, for my power is made perfect in weakness." Therefore I will boast all the more gladly about my weaknesses, so that Christ's power may rest on me. That is why, for Christ's sake, I delight in weaknesses, in insults, in hardships, in persecutions, in difficulties. For when I am weak, then I am strong. (2 Cor 12:7–10)

Pastors need to live lives resting in the Lord. This is a "be still and know that I am God" stance (Ps 46:10). I spent so much time working hard for God! I needed, as Pete Scazzero says, to be with God before I engage in activity for God.[21] I needed to come to the place where I realized before anything else that I am a child of God. To say "Abba" and to be that loved prodigal son.[22] It began to free me up. I was still driven. But my core changed. Richard Rohr writes,

> I am convinced that the Book of Jonah can best be read as God moving someone from a mere religious job, role, or career to an actual sense of personal call or destiny. . . . It takes being "swallowed by a beast" and taken into a dark place of nesting and nourishing that normally allows you to move to that deeper place called

21. Scazzero, *Emotionally Healthy Leader*, 121.

22. See Manning, *Abba's Child*; Nouwen, *Return of Prodigal Son*.

> personal vocation. You could describe it as moving from being ego driven to being soul drawn. The energy is very different. It comes quietly and generously from within you, and you do not look for payment, reward, or advancement because you have found your soul gift. You have to do it, or you are not you![23]

HOW DOES THIS GET LIVED OUT?

Remember when you first sensed that call to ministry? There is nothing more you wanted to do. Over time that sense of joy can fade. Whatever your role—pastor, missionary, organizational and ministry leader—ministry takes a toll on our lives. Trouble and disaster are seen not only in the meltdown of our externalized lives but also with a growing incongruity between how we present ourselves to others and what we are like on the inside.[24] If we are not careful, ministry—this task that we once loved—will kill us: emotionally, spiritually, relationally, and physically.

A friend of mine who is in charge of the care and discipline of pastors in the Evangelical Covenant Church notes this formula for disaster for clergy:

> Depletion + Isolation + Conflict = Significant Trouble

We can't do anything about conflict. It is a part of our lives as leaders, but we can order our lives so that we are not depleted or isolated. The place that sometimes brings troubles and conflicts our way is also the place where we develop, by Christ's power, into Christoformity. How do we do this? Here are some practices that we can integrate into our lives to keep the joy of ministry.

Abide

We need to stay connected to Jesus Christ as branches to the vine ("I am the vine; you are the branches. If you remain in me and I in you, you will bear much fruit; apart from me you can do nothing" [John 15:5]). Our strength ultimately comes from the Lord. We need to remain in him. We are people who humble ourselves and pick up the cross.

23. Rohr, *Lever and Place*, loc. 1397 of 1599.

24. Rich Villodas says, "Living well is about congruence, integrity, and, most importantly, love" (in Peterson, *On Living Well*, x).

David Thornburg calls this the cave. The cave represents the private, introspective space where we retreat to think, reflect, and transform knowledge into belief. It's where we go to process, recharge, and deepen our spiritual and emotional health. Leadership begins here; by carving out time for solitude and reflection, we connect with our deeper purpose. The cave is where we nurture our sacred space with God and cultivate the practice of spiritual reflection.[25]

Question: Where do you go for solitude and reflection?

So,

- Set aside time on a regular basis to read Scripture, to pray, to reflect, to confess. Strive to know Jesus better and become more like him.
- Engage with others in worship. Let corporate time hearing the word and gathering at the table nourish your life.
- Find a place, beyond your ministry context, to serve others. Don't be the leader or the organizer. Just slow down and care for others. Ministry to strangers, to the least of these, will change you.
- Remember back to your call to ministry. Write that story down. Recall what it was like when the Lord placed his hand on your life. What were the Lord's promises to you? Frederick Buechner reminds us, "By and large a good rule for finding out is this: the kind of work God usually calls you to is the kind of work (a) that you need most to do and (b) that the world most needs to have done. . . . The place God calls you to is the place where your deep gladness and the world's deep hunger meet."[26] How does that play out for you? When do you feel most alive? How do your passions align with the needs of the world around you?

25. David Thornburg, a visionary in educational technology, on three archetypal learning spaces: the cave, the campfire, and the watering hole. These spaces are identified in Thornburg, *From Campfire to Holodeck*; as cited in Bevins and Dunwoody, *Healthy Rhythms for Leaders*, 79-80.

26. Buechner, *Wishful Thinking*, 118–19. See Pemberton, "Frederick Buechner on Calling"; Bevins and Dunwoody, *Healthy Rhythms for Leaders*.

Breathe

We need to take time away from the busyness of life. Sometimes we just need to stop and get beyond the rat race. This is the Sabbath principle. This is where we have a chance to breathe. Jesus models this: "Very early in the morning, while it was still dark, Jesus got up, left the house and went off to a solitary place, where he prayed" (Mark 1:35).

We need space in our lives that is different. In the midst of each day, we need Sabbath time. Certainly, once a week, we need to stop working. We need to get off the treadmill of people pleasing and trying to prove our worth to God and ourselves. We need to just stop. One day in our lives should be different from the other six. Eugene Peterson says one day should be spent praying and playing.[27]

We handle stress better when we have a sense of confidence in God. Sabbath living helps us to center on lives in God, rather than in our activities and our doing. Here are some ways that will help us breathe:

- Recreate. Do something that is fun, that you can immerse yourself in. This is not ministry related; engage in activities that bring joy. Hike, run, play golf, kayak, garden, rock climb, bike—do something,
- Laugh. Laughter is very good for us! Find things that make you laugh and shake to your core.
- Get a pet!
- Take care of your body—pay attention to what you eat; get a good amount of sleep; exercise. We are not indestructible.
- Move beyond the clamor. Find quiet places in your life, away from computers and cell phones and people. Silence is not the absence of sound but the absence of noise.
- Go on a retreat. All by yourself. Without your cell phone. Walk, sit. Pray. Listen. Just turn off everything from your normal life.
- And really make one day of the week a Sabbath. Sabbath is too often the one command we are proud to break. Stop working! Sabbath is an essential practice for Christians, and this is especially true and difficult for ministry leaders. This practice alone can transform our ministry and our lives. It changes our stance in life. It is a practice that asserts

27. Peterson, *Pastor*, 220, 310.

in real time that "God is God, and I am not." It is a way of following Ps 46: "Be still, and know that I am God."

Practicing Sabbath reorients our life for the better. It confesses that:

- We are not necessary. Sabbath living declares my worth is not in what I do (1 Cor 3).
- We are not in control. Sabbath living declares God is God, and I am not (Ps 46; 2 Cor 12).
- We are not indestructible. Sabbath living declares that we are human and finite and fragile (1 Cor 6:19–20).

In living a Sabbath lifestyle, we hear Jesus's words: "Come to me, all you who are weary and burdened, and I will give you rest. Take my yoke upon you and learn from me, for I am gentle and humble in heart, and you will find rest for your souls. For my yoke is easy and my burden is light" (Matt 11:28).

Connect

We need to have good people circling around us. Whatever our personality, whether we are extroverted or introverted, in a way that works for us, we need to connect with others ("Just as a body, though one, has many parts, but all its many parts form one body, so it is with Christ" [1 Cor 12:5]).

To continue David Thornburg's analogy, connection happens at the campfire and the watering hole. The campfire is where we gather to learn from others, particularly mentors or coaches. Just like ancient cultures passed wisdom through storytelling around the fire, we too need the guidance of those who have walked before us. As leaders, we must prioritize having wise guides—coaches, spiritual directors, or trusted mentors—who can provide insight and help us navigate our own leadership journeys.

Question: Who are the mentors and coaches you are learning from?

The watering hole is the informal space of peer-driven learning. It's where we share ideas and experiences and support one another. This space allows us to teach and learn simultaneously, promoting a sense of shared culture and collaboration. As leaders, creating a coaching culture in our teams and organizations is vital, and the watering hole is where this collaboration and mutual growth happen.

Question: How are you engaging with peers to exchange ideas and grow together?

Consider the following ways to surround yourself with people who will walk with you through your life journey:

- Develop a small group of trusted friends. These are people who love you and care for you—not because of your job or your title. These are people you can vent to and confide in, who will say the hard things to you, and with whom you can just hang out and laugh, cry, or doubt and wonder. We need what Matt Bloom calls backstage people in our lives. These are the people who support and sustain us when we are "offstage," when we are not doing the work of ministry. These are the people with whom we can simply be ourselves, as raw and authentic as it might be. These are our companions, mentors, and wise guides.[28]
- Develop relationships in a faith community. We live our lives with others. Engage in the social aspects of church. Enjoy ministry colleagues. Be a part of a small group where you can share honestly with other ministry leaders.
- Be a lifelong learner. Keep stretching your thinking and your ministry skills. Read books and lots of kinds of books. Take a class. Get another degree. Better yourself. It will impact your life and your work for good. Learn a new language. Learn to play a musical instrument. Travel. All of these (and more) broaden your world.
- Pay attention to your family. They need your best, not what is left over. These are the most important relationships, so nurture them.
- As much as you can, create a satisfying work environment. A satisfying job is critical to your well-being. Develop a good attitude. Better yourself. Push yourself to do your work well and to make a difference. One study has found that people find satisfaction in their work when they have job resources such as supportive mentors, ongoing personal and skill development, and a sense of autonomy in their work.
- Love your congregation. Love the place where you serve. Allow your congregation to love you. Sometimes this is not easy, but to the best of your ability, and with the Lord's help, strive for affection toward your congregation. Dietrich Bonhoeffer writes words that are hard to live

28. Bloom, "'Stages' of Ministry."

> up to, but are worth noting: "A pastor should never complain about his congregation, certainly never to other people, but also not to God. A congregation has not been entrusted to him in order that he should become its accuser before God and men."[29]

Ministry always emerges out of who we are. In order to serve well, we must pay attention to our insides. It has been said, "When wealth is lost, nothing is lost. When health is lost, something is lost. When character is lost, everything is lost."[30]

Pastors strive to be people of character, who have good hearts. As I wrote previously, the recipe for disaster in our lives is *depletion + isolation + conflict = significant trouble*. The path toward ministering well and finishing well is:

abide (in Christ)—breathe (in still spaces)—connect (with others)

I pray that you will continue to serve well in the world and attend to your life. Do this for yourself and for those entrusted to your care.

29. Bonhoeffer, *Life Together*, 29–30.

30. These words are widely attributed to Billy Graham but without a clear published source.

Conclusion

The Spirit of Christ driving the *missio Dei* disturbs the system to the core. Newbigin reminds us that the mission of the church is the "radioactive fallout" of "an explosion of joy."[1] As the church is receptive to and captivated by the Spirit, something new begins to occur. This reality empowers the church in mission, in many different shapes and forms in this era and every era.

The church must change. The church has been moved to the margins of culture. This marginality creates disruption but also provides an opportunity for new mission. This new mission will most often begin at the innovative, missionally heretical fringes of the church but will influence toward the center. This renewed center will send ripples of renewal out to the fringes and then back toward the center again. This is not a time for the timid. The church of the future will be more organic than machinelike. It will have characteristics that are more postmodern than modern. It will be flatter, more dynamic, and uncertain.

In Luke 10, Jesus gives instructions to the seventy as they were sent out in mission. Based on this passage, Walter Brueggemann reminds us of the mission of the church. First, the church risks going out among wolves. This is a different world that we are a part of. It is not to be feared; it is to be entered into with courage. The church steps out into the unknown. Second, the church travels light. The heavy institution does not characterize the future church. The church must emerge fluid, liquid, organic, and changing. Third, the church acts. The church brings healing and blessing to the world. The church is a servant. As it travels, it does good, offering forgiveness and the promise of transformation. Fourth, the church talks. The church is engaged in the activity of proclamation, critique, informing, and listening. The church proclaims good news that transforms the faith

1. Newbigin, *Gospel in Pluralist Society*, 127.

community and the world, offering a new identity and a new way of living. The church proclaims, lives out, and ushers in the reign of God.[2]

A lot of what has been assumed in a Christendom world will now be questioned in a post-Christendom world. If you are faint of heart, beware. While a reimagining of the church and implementing new practices will be the cause for debate, critique, and even ridicule, the future of the mission of God in the world demands that the church be willing to move in new directions and encourage an ecclesial environment that sees the emergence of new structures.

The church can become fire-like. The church can shake off its modernistic, Christendom cloak. Our souls can blaze anew with missional imaginations. The church of the future will engage culture in new and vital ways, and the world will be blessed.

> So, bring on the insecurity, the disruptions, and the fire.
> So that the church of Jesus Christ might be more than it is today.
> To the glory of God.

2. Brueggemann, *Word That Redescribes World*, 100.

A Final Word

A SERMON FROM MARK 4: JESUS IS IN THE BOAT[1]

> As evening came, Jesus said to his disciples, "Let's cross to the other side of the lake." So they took Jesus in the boat and started out, leaving the crowds behind (although other boats followed). But soon a fierce storm came up. High waves were breaking into the boat, and it began to fill with water. Jesus was sleeping at the back of the boat with his head on a cushion. The disciples woke him up, shouting, "Teacher, don't you care that we're going to drown?" When Jesus woke up, he rebuked the wind and said to the waves, "Silence! Be still!" Suddenly the wind stopped, and there was a great calm. Then he asked them, "Why are you afraid? Do you still have no faith?" The disciples were absolutely terrified. "Who is this man?" they asked each other. "Even the wind and waves obey him!" (Mark 4:35–41)

The love of Christ compels us to be on mission in this new season in new ways. It is a journey, and it will not be an easy journey. On any journey the destination is important, but traveling to that destination, as well as the companions along the way, is also important.

Since congregations should be more like gardens than machines, ministry leaders engage in the missional journey from a new perspective. This changes the way leaders participate in ministry and with each other. This is not an easy journey. There will be risks and disappointments but also

1. From my sermon preached for Fuller Theological Seminary's baccalaureate on June 3, 2015: Fredrickson, "Let Us Cross Over."

the joy of seeing ministry flourish in new ways—for God's glory and the neighbors' good!

Along the way on the journey, lessons are learned from successes and failures. Relationships are forged. Memories are created. Imaginations are inspired. Mistakes are made, and that is expected. And there might even be a bit of mischief.

When we lived in California, I commuted forty miles each way from Ventura County to Fuller Seminary in Pasadena. I knew where cell service was poor and where a call would drop. I knew where traffic bottlenecks and where police officers perched waiting for speeders. It wasn't an epic journey; it was just a commute.

A journey has a different feel. Whether a road trip, backpacking with friends, or a cross-country family vacation, a journey has a sense of purpose and adventure. Journeys are exciting because they push us out of our comfort zone, into the unknown and the unfamiliar. There is uncertainty and maybe even a sense of wonder. And our lives get changed. Because of the journey, we will never be the same.

Jesus calls us out of our comfort zone and onto a risky path of adventure and mission. Jesus meets us in the midst of storms, however they arise in our lives, and promises to be with us. Beyond the storm, in the midst of the storm, is the reality and presence of Jesus Christ our resurrected and living Lord. And this Jesus changes everything.

In this text Jesus is calling his disciples on a journey with the invitation: Let's cross to the other side of the lake. It is a call to discipleship and mission. Once again Jesus is saying, "Follow me!" Jesus has been working, teaching, and healing on the west side of the Sea of Galilee. This is the Jewish side—the familiar side. He has done great work here. It is satisfying work, but the gospel work must continue. The gospel cannot be kept in the realm of the safe and the known and comfortable. So Jesus calls his disciples to venture into the unknown, the untested, and the unfamiliar. They cross over into gentile territory.

The disciples launched out with Jesus on the Sea of Galilee and ran into a storm. Sudden, violent storms are well known on the lake. Storms drive waves over the sides of the boat, filling the boat with water. When a storm hits at night, like this one, it is even more dangerous and frightening.

Some of Jesus's disciples were seasoned, experienced fisherman. But when this evening storm arose, they were terrified. The text says a fierce storm came up. High waves were breaking into the boat, and it began to fill with water. Jesus was sleeping at the back of the boat with his head on a cushion.

Do you catch this? Jesus said, "Let's cross to the other side." The disciples obey. And they get caught in a terrible storm. It's a storm that threatens their lives. And Jesus is asleep in the back of the boat. The disciples wake him up with shouting! "Teacher, don't you care that we're going to drown?" Ever feel like that? Jesus, don't you care? The storm rages, and Jesus is napping.

Jesus gets up. He rises to his full height. He sees the wind and the waves. And he commands and rebukes the wind and the sea: "Silence, be still!" And the wind settled down and there was a great calm. Jesus asked, "Why are you afraid? Do you still have no faith?"

We can imagine the disciples are wide eyed. Relieved that they are safe. Frightened and confused. Uncertain of what to do. What just happened? The wind and the seas obey him? Their fear of the storm now becomes a fear and awe of Jesus! In wonderment they ask, who is this? This is more than a mere man. This is a glimpse of God the Creator as the Spirit hovered over the surface of the waters.

We are always people on mission. Jesus said to his disciples, "Let us go to the other side of the lake." The gospel cannot be contained. The word keeps pressing out, moving forward. With Paul we say, "I am not ashamed of the gospel" (Rom 1:16). There is an urgency to share the news of Jesus. Eugene Peterson says, "Church is the appointed gathering of named people in particular places who practice a life of resurrection in a world in which death gets the biggest headlines."[2]

A boat has been a symbol for the church from its earliest days. Like the fish symbol, the image of a boat was an undercover way to identify believers and congregations in times of persecution. The church has been and always will be a storm-tossed boat with the cross for a mast.

The first readers of this gospel were Christian communities. This book was not just a set of stories about Jesus. It was also a manual for discipleship and mission. The first readers would have caught the message: the good news of Jesus is not just for Jews; it is also for gentiles. Jesus's followers must get in the boat and go to the other side. The gospel is always extending:

> To the lost, the marginalized, the unclean,
> The overlooked, the ignored,
> The different, the abandoned, the misfits, the judged.

2. Peterson, *Practice Resurrection*, 3.

"Let us go to the other side" is the press of Jesus on us still, as a church, as followers of Jesus. The gospel is always extending, even when it is uncomfortable.

This is no cruise ship.[3] We are not passengers on vacation. We are the crew. We don't sit back waiting to be serve or entertained. We work. We don't go off to our own staterooms to relax or nap. We are together, working. We are the body of Christ: one Lord, one faith, one baptism, one meal we share. We worship together, we eat together, we work together, we cry, and we laugh together. We love one another. We are in the Jesus boat. We are family, sisters and brothers.

Jesus calls us into the boat. We don't stay safely on the shore or at the dock. The boat is meant for sailing. We get in the boat even if the message will not be received well, even if there is persecution, even if there are storms. We get in the boat even though stepping out on mission with Jesus is risky, because we have good news to share. We hear Jesus say, "Let's go to the other side." And we go.

The Celtic monks and missionaries of Ireland and Britain in the fifth and sixth centuries entered into what they called the White Martyrdom. They would get into little boats. They would break through the surf. They set out on the ocean, not knowing where they were going. Waves and currents would take them to new landing places, and in those new places they would share the gospel and plant new Christian communities.

Jesus says to every congregation, and to you, "Step out in mission. Let's cross over to the other side." Stepping into the boat sets us on a new course, a journey with elements of adventure and wonder.

> Question: What does that crossing over to the other side look like for you personally, and for your congregation? Where is the Lord calling you?

This gospel story reminds us that in the midst of the storms in our lives, Jesus is present. The wind is howling—gale-force winds. The waves beat against your life, your ministry, and your congregation. You are afraid you will drown. Where are you beaten down? Fears on the outside, struggles within. Whatever storm you are facing today, and will be facing on the journey ahead, the Lord is with you—even if it seems he is asleep in the back of the boat. Isaiah 43 reminds us,

3. For more on this analogy, see Jethani, *Churches Became Cruise Ships*.

But now, says the Lord—
the one who created you, Jacob,
the one who formed you, Israel:
Don't fear, for I have redeemed you;
I have called you by name; you are mine.
When you pass through the waters, I will be with you;
when through the rivers, they won't sweep over you.
When you walk through the fire, you won't be scorched
and flame won't burn you.
I am the Lord your God,
the holy one of Israel, your savior. (Isa 43:1–3 CEB)

This is good news! This is a promise to us! Your boat, your life, your church, takes on water. It feels like more than you can handle: "O God, thy sea is so great, and my boat is so small."[4] But you are not alone! Jesus is in the boat. And we trust. Jesus says, "Quiet . . . be still." And there is peace. Cling to that today.

This passage is about being on a missional journey—and encountering storms. It is also about the wonder of seeing and following Jesus in the midst of it all. Jesus calls you to cross over to the other side. And you go. Why? Because Jesus is in the boat!

You sense the press of God on your life—to live for him in new ways in your life, your ministry, your neighborhood, your congregation. You hear Jesus say, "Let's cross over to the other side. Follow me." And you do. Why? Because Jesus is in the boat.

You cross over, and sometimes storms will rage—and you will be afraid and feel alone and maybe doubt, but it's okay. Why? Because underneath it all, through it all, you know that Jesus is in the boat.

The way forward may be uncomfortable. It may be risky and uncertain. But you go anyway. Why? Because Jesus is in the boat.

Saint Brendan was one of those fifth-century Celtic monks who set sail in a small boat of wood and ox hide from Ireland and ended up in Newfoundland. He heard the Lord say, "Let's go to the other side, wherever that might be, whatever it cost"—and he went. In the midst of the storms of life and ministry, he trusted the Lord. This is his prayer—and it can be our prayer. For your lives and for your church:

4. Winfred Ernest Garrison; as adapted in Baxter, "Prayer of Breton Fishermen." The original words are "Thy sea, O God, so great / My boat so small."

Help me to journey beyond the familiar
and into the unknown.
Give me the faith to leave old ways
and break fresh ground with You.

Christ of the mysteries, I trust You
to be stronger than each storm within me.
I will trust in the darkness and know
that my times, even now, are in Your hand.
Tune my spirit to the music of heaven,
and somehow, make my obedience count for You.[5]

Jesus calls us to follow him, to cross over to the other side. We are the church on mission. We are a Jesus boat—the Lord is with us. Through every storm, with every hard command. He says in the midst of it all, "Quiet! Be still!" We cling to each other: on mission, in the storms. And we trust and follow and worship him—no matter what—because Jesus is in the boat!

In 2 Cor 4, Paul writes these words, "Therefore, since God in his mercy has given us this ministry we never give up." Being a ministry leader is a difficult call at times. Be we carry on. We continue to preach, witness, and proclaim good news. We care and shepherd. We lead and encourage new imaginations. We offer counsel and hospitality. We work to see God's mission expand. We seek to shine the light on injustice and work to set the world right in Jesus's name.

You do this work in season and out of season—this is the calling on your life. The Lord has grabbed your life—this is what you do. You serve faithfully, hoping for great fruitfulness. You are aware of the Lord's presence and power on your life

And so—never give up! In times of abundance *and* scarcity—never give up. When you have energy *and* when you are fatigued—never give up. When you enjoy the noise of crowds *and* when you feel very alone—never give up. When many find favor with others in what you do *and* when you experience conflict—never give up. When you are hopeful *and* when you despair—never give up.

It's the best life there is.

5. As quoted in Filz, "Inspiring Prayer."

Appendix

TABLE AND EUCHARIST: TWO KEY PRACTICES FOR THE CHURCH ON MISSION

Hospitality and the Lord's Table point toward a kingdom reality. These two key overlapping practices impact a congregation and set it up to be a new type of church on mission, within the congregation and beyond. They change how we are church and give a glimpse of what is envisioned in the worldwide, diverse kingdom of God.

Table fellowship was historically a central venue for living out the reign of God in the midst of ordinary life, and it can continue to be an affirming and challenging image and practice of mission today. Bevans and Schroeder suggest there are three "tables" of fellowship:

- The dining room table of the domestic church
- The eucharistic table of the parish community
- The worldwide table of God's diverse peoples[1]

Bonhoeffer writes: "The Scriptures speak of three kinds of community at the table that Jesus keeps with his own: the daily breaking of bread together at meals, the breaking of bread together at the Lord's Supper, and the final breaking of bread together in the reign of God. But in all three, the one thing that counts is that 'their eyes were opened and they recognized him.'"[2]

1. Bevans and Schroeder, *Prophetic Dialogue*, loc. 2077–78 of 3767.
2. Bonhoeffer, *Life Together*, 72.

Hospitality

A key practice within a congregation is hospitality. Hospitality is about how the church relates to each other and to the world. As a congregation, God's people must practice being faithful and welcoming.

Hospitality is deeper than friendliness. "Through the lens of Christian faith, hospitality becomes a counterculture expression of love that elevates us above fear of the 'other' and compels us to welcome the stranger."[3] We extend our hands to others, accepting them into the fellowship of the church. We extend grace. Hospitality—being at table with others—is a primary mark of the ministry of Jesus. He was always eating with others![4] The table in homes can be a metaphor and a reality for extending the love of Jesus.

> Jesus' mission was to proclaim, serve, and witness to God's Reign of love, salvation, and justice. In the process, Jesus both affirmed and confronted certain aspects of his own context. Table fellowship was a central venue for serving the Reign of God, and it can continue to be an affirming and challenging image and practice of mission today.[5]

Hospitality is a word that has become domesticated, but it can be a wonderful and powerful way to share the love of Jesus. It has a strong moral character. At the table, we reach out to others. We include those who are different from us. We engage in conversation. We learn from each other. In the words of Christine Pohl, two dynamics are at work: the needy guest and the gracious host, and the needy host and the gifting guest.[6] Hospitality changes everyone for the better. As an Irish proverb states, "It is in the shelter of each other that the people live." Or in the words of Robert Frost, "Home is the place where, when you have to go there, / They have to take you in."[7]

3. Rivers, "Witness of Hospitality," para. 1.

4. Table fellowship is seen throughout Luke's Gospel: the banquet in Levi's home (5:27–32), the dinner at Simon's home (7:36–50), feeding the five thousand (9:10–17), hospitality at Mary and Martha's home (10:38–42), the dinner at a Pharisee's home (11:37–52), a Sabbath meal at a Pharisee's home (14:1–24), hospitality at the home of Zacchaeus (19:1–10), the Last Supper (22:14–38), breaking bread together (24:28–32), and the meal with the Eleven (24:36–43).

5. Bevans and Schroeder, *Prophetic Dialogue*, loc. 1936 of 3767.

6. Pohl, *Making Room*, loc. 201 of 2536.

7. R. Frost, "Death of Hired Man."

Hospitality is a metaphor, but it is also a very tangible practice. Everyone can engage in dining room table fellowship. One does not need to be a good cook! We can gather at this hospitality table in homes, restaurants, or in a park. We have parties. We share drinks. We provide meals. Something good happens when we eat together. "Food is a language of care," writes Shauna Niequist, "the thing we do when traditional language fails."[8] Food is subtle and powerful. In the ordinary, life is enriched. Rachel Held Evans, reflecting on the difficult decision she and her husband made to leave their congregation, writes,

> We crossed the parking lot, which still smelled of fresh asphalt, and climbed into the safety of our car. As soon as the doors shut, I put my head in my hands and cried, startled to tears by the selfishness of my own thoughts: Who will bring us casseroles when we have a baby?[9]

This is not selfishness. This is a recognition that at the critical and wonderful moments in life, we need people around us to care for us and to celebrate with us. And that attention often involves food! Gathering, eating, and sharing is lovingly powerful.

At the table with others, through hospitality, we live out what the gospel is to be in the congregation, in our neighborhoods, and in the world. It is here that we experience the mystery and the messiness of church. In simple acts of hospitality, the church becomes a sign, instrument, and foretaste of the kingdom of God. In simple acts of hospitality, the church lives out Gal 3:28: "There is neither Jew nor Gentile, neither slave nor free, nor is there male and female, for you are all one in Christ Jesus." As has been said: don't build walls, but build longer tables.

The Lord's Table

Within a congregation, the Lord's Table can be a regular practice that changes the mood of a congregation.[10] The Lord's Supper is the sacrament that remembers and enacts the work of Christ on the cross. The Lord's Table reminds us of the presence of Christ among us and our unity as

8. As quoted in Evans, *Searching for Sunday*, 154.
9. Evans, *Searching for Sunday*, 83.
10. Fredrickson, "Church at Table."

sisters and brothers in Christ.[11] Whenever two or three gather in the name of Jesus, the Lord promises to be present (Matt 18:20). The psalmist proclaims: "How good and pleasant it is when God's people live together in unity!" (Ps 133:1). But that is not always easy.

Struggles toward unity also aren't something new. A quick glance through Paul's letters in the New Testament shows that disagreements were a part of congregational life then as well. The Corinthian church was dealing with issues of immorality, doctrinal disputes, and celebrity pastors. The Philippian church was living though a disagreement between two people in the congregation. Paul writes, "I plead with Euodia and I plead with Syntyche to be of the same mind in the Lord" (Phil 4:2). Church people have disagreements that can turn contentious. The church is a mystery, and it is also messy. It always has been that way.

In our common baptism, we are to strive toward unity. It is the prayer of our Lord: "I am praying not only for these disciples but also for all who will ever believe in me through their message. I pray that they will all be one, just as you and I are one—as you are in me, Father, and I am in you. And may they be in us so that the world will believe you sent me" (John 17:20–21 NLT). This is the apostle Paul's hope and admonition:

> Therefore I, a prisoner for serving the Lord, beg you to lead a life worthy of your calling, for you have been called by God. Always be humble and gentle. Be patient with each other, making allowance for each other's faults because of your love. Make every effort to keep yourselves united in the Spirit, binding yourselves together with peace. For there is one body and one Spirit, just as you have been called to one glorious hope for the future.
>
> There is one Lord, one faith, one baptism, one God and Father of all, who is over all, in all, and living through all. (Eph 4:1–6 NLT)

Paul's primary designation for followers of Jesus is brothers and sisters. Scot McKnight notes that "the idea of siblingship is the dominant self-understanding and self-designation of the church.[12] We are siblings with each other. We are family: not associates, neighbors, or merely friends. We are family.

11. The Lord's Table, in my thinking, also replaces the altar call in some traditions. As people receive the bread and the wine, it is an opportunity to make a declaration of following the ways of Jesus, and trusting in the work of the cross for them.

12. McKnight, *Pastor Paul*, 61.

We bring the best and the most challenging aspects of family into our life together. At our best and at our worst, we are committed to each other. We are wonderfully stuck with each other. We have a bond that is so firm that we must live lives committed to each other even when there are disagreements. This connection is a reality because we are in Christ. Christ is present in our congregations. Dietrich Bonhoeffer writes,

> Christian community means community through Jesus Christ and in Jesus Christ. There is no Christian community that is more than this, and none that is less than this. Whether it be a brief, single encounter or the daily community of many years, Christian community is solely this. We belong to one another only through and in Jesus Christ.[13]

We are called to peace: "Let the peace of Christ rule in your hearts, since as members of one body you were called to peace. And be thankful" (Col 3:15). We are committed to each other, even when forces in the church and in our society seek to bring divisiveness and polarization. We are family. We are sisters and brothers in the Lord. That changes the way that we do our lives together.

In a local congregation, we will have differences of opinions, even disagreements. Siblings do. That is okay. But Christ is present in our midst, so we remain connected to each other: open minded, humble, and courageous.[14] Christopher Smith notes, "Too many churches remain shallow and immature because they go to great lengths to avoid the tiniest semblance of disagreement."[15] Our disagreements do not need to become conflict. "Disagreements do not necessarily precipitate conflict. Rather, conflict is disagreement that has become insidious and is ripping a community apart. We find ourselves in conflict when we layer all sorts of sin and distrust on top of our disagreements."[16]

The Philippian church was experiencing dissention, a rift in the fellowship (Phil 4:1–3). Paul calls that congregation to unity in Christ by pointing to the humbling stance of Jesus.

> Therefore, if you have any encouragement from being united with Christ, if any comfort from his love, if any common sharing in

13. Bonhoeffer, *Life Together*, 31.
14. C. Smith, *How the Body Talks*, 148.
15. C. Smith, *How the Body Talks*, 149.
16. C. Smith, *How the Body Talks*, 144.

> the Spirit, if any tenderness and compassion, then make my joy complete by being like-minded, having the same love, being one in spirit and of one mind. Do nothing out of selfish ambition or vain conceit. Rather, in humility value others above yourselves, not looking to your own interests but each of you to the interests of the others. In your relationships with one another, have the same mindset as Christ Jesus: Who, being in very nature God, did not consider equality with God something to be used to his own advantage; rather, he made himself nothing by taking the very nature of a servant. (Phil 2:1–7)

At one point while I was pastoring my congregation, we entered into a lively and extended discussion about the role of women in ministry in our church. It was not an easy time for our church. The congregation, and its leaders, searched the Scriptures and our hearts and finally brought the matter up for a vote. The congregation affirmed that women could serve in all ministries of the church based on their calling and giftedness, and we hired a female associate pastor. One of the most vocal dissenters on this topic was a much-loved and respected layperson. Even though he strongly disagreed with the decision, he said: "My church has decided. I respect that decision, and will continue to participate and serve here. This is my church." That is a Christ-formed attitude, submitting to the Lord and to the congregation.

In the midst of troubles from without, and in the midst of difficulties and divisions that threaten us from within, how do we live out this type of life, being formed into the image of Christ? I suggest that the ongoing and thoughtful practice of meeting together at the Lord's Table reminds us that a congregation is made up of sisters and brothers in Christ, and it creates a mood where, by the Spirit, we live into this reality. Through this meal, we affirm the presence of the crucified and risen Christ in our midst and our commitment to live as sisters and brothers in our lives together. The *Covenant Book of Worship* offers this invitation to the table:

> Come to this sacred table, not because you must, but because you may; come to testify not that you are righteous, but that you sincerely love our Lord Jesus Christ and desire to be his true disciples; come not because you are strong, but because you are weak; not because you have any claim on the grace of God, but because in your frailty and sin you stand in constant need of God's mercy and help; come, not to express an opinion, but to seek God's presence and pray for the Spirit.[17]

17. Evangelical Covenant Church, *Covenant Book of Worship*, loc. 3759–62 of 11,205.

At the Lord's Table, we remember the work of Jesus on the cross. This work tears down walls that divide us (Eph 2:14–16). At the Lord's Table, we are reminded that we are one body in Christ (1 Cor 11:33; 12:12–13). The *Covenant Book of Worship* states:

> Is not the bread that we break a participation in the body of Christ? Because there is one loaf, we, who are many, are one body, for we all partake of the one loaf.[18]

As we share in the Lord's Supper, we are reminded of the Last Supper where Jesus washes the disciple's feet (John 13:1–17). Jesus is our model in this humbling act: "Do you see what I was doing?" The Lord's Supper reminds us that we are to submit to each other. We confess our sins to each other. At the table we seek reconciliation with each other, forgiveness, and restoration. Where there have been misunderstandings, hurt, and harm, we make it right (Matt 5:23–24; 18:15–20). As with broken bones, we acknowledge the pain caused by fractures. As a body, we work to align the fractured parts. As sisters and brothers, we support the fracture while it heals.[19] David Fitch writes,

> The church, however, comes together around the presence of the living God. This presence comes as an overflowing gift through the incarnate Christ becoming present by the Spirit among this people. This presence offers forgiveness, reconciliation, healing, and renewal by the Spirit. It transforms relationships in a face-to-face encounter. The reality of his fullness is present wherever we gather because he comes in flesh and blood, the body and blood, broken and raised for all. Its resources are infinite because God is infinite. Its core is full and unending. This politic shapes us as a peaceful people, a people of invitation and generosity to the world, a people beyond enemies, a church beyond us vs. them.[20]

I'm not suggesting that this will be easy, but gathering together at the Lord's Table over time (and being tested in the difficult times) holds the promise of fostering a new culture in a congregation where we see each other as sisters and brothers in Christ. Bonhoeffer writes,

> The day of the Lord's Supper is a joyous occasion for the Christian community. Reconciled in their hearts with God and one another,

18. Evangelical Covenant Church, *Covenant Book of Worship*, loc. 3888–89 of 11,205.
19. C. Smith, *How the Body Talks*, 150–61.
20. Fitch, *Church of Us vs. Them*, 164.

> the community of faith receives the gift of Jesus Christ's body and blood, therein receiving forgiveness, new life, and salvation. New community with God and one another is given to it. The community of the holy Lord's Supper is above all the fulfillment of Christian community.[21]

The Lord's Table shapes how we live our lives with each other in worship, in witness, and as a community. It transforms every aspect of our congregational life. The key elements of hospitality and the Eucharist overlap and are lived out in various areas of congregational life.

In Small Groups

This is the kitchen table of our congregations. At this table, we get to know and trust each other. Here, we eat together, read Scripture together, pray together, share and honor our stories, and perhaps share the Eucharist. Here, we risk and more deeply share our lives, confess our sins, and become accountable to each other. At this table, we learn to listen. "Just as our love for God begins with listening to God's Word, the beginning of love for other Christians is learning to listen to them."[22] This table extends out as smaller groups of people engage in the wider world. Being gracious in our speech and Christlike in our actions (Phil 2:15; Col 4:5–6; 1 Pet 3:15), neighbors are invited to share in meals and catch glimpses of the gospel. As Michael Green would say, we "gossip the gospel."[23] Working side by side, people get to know each other informally and serve in the community in the Lord's name. At this table, we also experiment on how to discuss and discern controversial matters. We are together seeking what it means to follow Christ in all situations.

It won't always be easy. Mistakes will be made. The community will need to ask for forgiveness and for a reset. But we are sisters and brothers, so we work through our difficulties. We always remember the table. Smith

21. Bonhoeffer, *Life Together*, 118.

22. Bonhoeffer, *Life Together*, 98.

23. Green, *Evangelism in Early Church*, 173. Green continues, "This must often have been not formal preaching, but the informal chattering to friends and chance acquaintances, in homes and wine shops, on walks, and around market stalls. They were everywhere gossiping the gospel; they did it naturally, enthusiastically, and with the conviction of those who are not paid to say that sort of thing. Consequently, they were taken seriously, and the movement spread." See also M. Frost, *Surprise the World*; Kreider, *Patient Ferment of Church*.

comments: "A baby is not born with the capability to walk, let alone walk a tightrope. Similarly, we need to develop some skill, grace, trust, and maturity before we expect to walk the tightrope of highly charged questions without repeatedly tumbling and endangering the life of our body."[24]

In Pastoral Leadership

The preaching table is a significant part of a congregation's life together. The word is preached "in season and out of season" (2 Tim 4:2). The way the word is proclaimed shapes a congregation. Pastors and others proclaiming the word from the pulpit and in other venues serve as priests and prophets. They comfort, encourage, guide, challenge, and even disturb the congregation toward Christoformity. They do this, not from a distance, but as those among their people. The apostle Paul saw his work among the church in Thessalonica as children, mothers, and fathers (1 Thess 2:7–12). Pope Francis encourages clergy to have the smell of sheep.[25] The Christ-formed life portrayed in the Lord's Supper characterizes the life of ministry leaders. The apostle Peter reminds pastors how they are to live out their calling in a congregation:

> To the elders among you, I appeal as a fellow elder and a witness of Christ's sufferings who also will share in the glory to be revealed: Be shepherds of God's flock that is under your care, watching over them—not because you must, but because you are willing, as God wants you to be; not pursuing dishonest gain, but eager to serve; not lording it over those entrusted to you, but being examples to the flock. And when the Chief Shepherd appears, you will receive the crown of glory that will never fade away. (1 Pet 5:1–4)

Pastors serve not only through the preaching table. They also model this servant life through other aspects of ministry: counseling, weddings, funerals, administration, and conversations.[26] As pastors do their work in this way, a congregation can be newly shaped. Pastors, remembering the table, are transformed as they carry out their tasks.

24. C. Smith, *How the Body Talks*, 49–50.

25. Francis, *Smell of the Sheep*, loc. 297 of 3304.

26. "Whether we realize it or not, every act of ministry reveals something of God. By act of ministry, I mean a sermon preached, a lesson taught, a marriage performed, counsel offered, any other word or act that people might construe as carrying God's blessing, warning, or judgment" (R. Anderson, *Soul of Ministry*, 7).

In Board Meetings and Congregational Meetings

Remembering the Lord's Table, the boardroom table is transformed. The mood of business sessions does not need to be contentious, but joyful. We do the business—the mission—of the church with one heart and mind. The Lord's Table reminds us how we are to act at the boardroom table and congregational meetings. Imagine church board meetings and congregational meetings as opportunities for dwelling in the word and listening to each other, praying, sharing our lives, expressing our concerns, and confessing our sins to each other as the mission of the church advances. Difficult decisions will have to be made. There will be disagreements. But approaching these matters in the spirit of the table, where we are reminded that we are connected to the Lord and to each other as sisters and brothers, changes the way we do our work.

Conclusion

The practice of gathering together at the table changes who we are as a congregation. In deeper ways, we become sisters and brothers in Christ. In the midst of our differences—even through our differences—we are one in Christ experiencing the peace of Christ, as we demonstrate the love of Christ. The Lord's Table is the practice of the church that reminds us of the way of Jesus, the way of emptying and humility—of Christoformity. A local congregation will begin to change as it incorporates these nurturing elements into its life together. It is a slow process, maybe unrecognizable as a congregation moves through it. Our children grow right before our eyes, but we don't notice it as we live with them daily. A garden moves from winter to spring in small increments, but looking back at photos over months and years, you notice the change.

Bibliography

Addison, Steve. *Movements That Change the World: Five Keys to Spreading the Gospel.* Downers Grove, IL: InterVarsity, 2011.

Allen, Roland. *The Spontaneous Expansion of the Church.* Grand Rapids: Eerdmans, 1962.

Alves, Rubem. *Tomorrow's Child: Imagination, Creativity, and the Rebirth of Culture.* New York: Harper & Row, 1972.

Anderson, Philip J. "The Covenant and the American Challenge: Restoring a Dynamic View of Identity and Pluralism." In *Amicus Dei: Essays on Faith and Friendship; Presented to Karl A. Olsson on His 75th Birthday*, edited by Philip J. Anderson, 109–47. Chicago: Covenant, 1988.

Anderson, Ray S. *An Emergent Theology for Emerging Churches.* Downers Grove, IL: IVP, 2006.

———. *The Shape of Practical Theology: Empowering Ministry with Theological Praxis.* Downers Grove, IL: IVP, 2006.

———. *The Soul of Ministry: Forming Leaders for God's People.* Louisville: Westminster John Knox, 1997.

Barnes, M. Craig. *Diary of a Pastor's Soul: The Holy Moments in a Life of Ministry.* Grand Rapids: Brazos, 2020.

Baxter, Ellen. "The Prayer of the Breton Fishermen: Finding Calm amid Life's Storms." Center for Healthy Churches, Nov. 4, 2024. https://chchurches.org/the-prayer-of-the-breton-fishermen/.

Bergquist, William. *The Postmodern Organization: Mastering the Art of Irreversible Change.* Jossey-Bass Business & Management Series. San Francisco: Jossey-Bass, 1993.

Bevans, Stephen B. "The Church as Creation of the Spirit: Unpacking a Missionary Image." *Missiology* 35 (2007) 5–21.

Bevans, Stephen B., and Roger P. Schroeder. *Prophetic Dialogue: Reflections on Christian Mission Today.* Maryknoll, NY: Orbis, 2012. Kindle.

Bevins, Winfield, and Mark Dunwoody. *Healthy Rhythms for Leaders: Cultivating Soul Care in Unseen Spaces.* Franklin, TN: Exponential, 2021.

Bartholomew, Craig. "5 Reasons to Read Wendell Berry Today." BibleMesh, July 28, 2022. https://biblemesh.com/blog/5-reasons-to-read-wendell-berry-today.

Bloom, Matt. "Research: The 'Stages' of Ministry." Thriving in Ministry, July 12, 2017. https://thrivinginministry.org/research-the-stages-of-ministry.

Bolsinger, Tod, and Markus Watson. *Spiritual Life and Leadership.* Episode 281, "Learning Our Way Forward." Aug. 12, 2025. https://podcasts.apple.com/us/podcast/281-learning-our-way-forward-a-quick-conversation/id1435252632?i=1000721625130.

Bolsinger, Tod E. *Canoeing the Mountains: Christian Leadership in Uncharted Territory.* Downers Grove, IL: IVP, 2015.

Bolz-Weber, Nadia. *Pastrix: The Cranky, Beautiful Faith of a Sinner & Saint.* New York: Jericho, 2013.

Bonhoeffer, Dietrich. *The Cost of Discipleship.* Translated by R. H. Fuller. Translation revised by Irmgard Booth. New York: Simon and Schuster, 1995.

———. *Ethics.* Translated by Neville Horton Smith. New York: Macmillan, 1955.

———. *Letters and Papers from Prison.* Edited by Eberhard Bethge et al. New York: Touchstone, 1997.

———. *Life Together.* Translated by John W. Doberstein. New York: Harper & Row, 1954.

———. *"Life Together" and "Prayerbook of the Bible."* Vol. 5 of *Dietrich Bonhoeffer Works.* Edited by Gerhard Ludwig Müller et al. Translated by Daniel W. Bloesch and James H. Burtness. Minneapolis: Fortress, 2004.

———. *Sanctorum Communio: A Theological Study of the Sociology of the Church.* Edited by Joachim von Soosten et al. Minneapolis: Fortress, 1998.

Bosch, David J. *Believing in the Future: Toward a Missiology of Western Culture.* Valley Forge, PA: Trinity, 1995.

———. *Transforming Mission: Paradigm Shifts in Theology of Mission.* Maryknoll, NY: Orbis, 1991.

Brafman, Ori, and Rod A. Beckstrom. *The Starfish and the Spider: The Unstoppable Power of Leaderless Organizations.* New York: Portfolio, 2006.

Branson, Mark Lau. *Memories, Hopes, and Conversations: Appreciative Inquiry and Congregational Change.* Herndon, VA: Alban Institute, 2004.

Briggs, J. R. *Fail: Finding Hope and Grace in the Midst of Ministry Failure.* Downers Grove, IL: IVP, 2014.

———. *Resilient Leaders.* Episode 25, "Are You Blasted?" Sept. 8, 2020. https://podcasts.apple.com/us/podcast/are-you-blasted/id1503152810?i=1000489981735.

Brisco, Brad. "The Welcome Rise of Co-Vocational Church Planters." Missio Alliance, Dec. 23, 2024. https://www.missioalliance.org/the-welcome-rise-of-co-vocational-church-planters/.

Brueggemann, Walter. *The Word That Redescribes the World: The Bible and Discipleship.* Minneapolis: Fortress, 2006.

Buechner, Frederick. *Wishful Thinking: A Theological ABC.* San Francisco: HarperCollins, 1993.

Bullock, Marion Wyvetta. "The Challenge of Developing Missional Agencies and the Implications for Leadership." In *The Missional Church and Denominations: Helping Congregations Develop a Missional Identity*, edited by Craig Van Gelder, 104–30. Grand Rapids: Eerdmans, 2008.

Callahan, Kennon L. *Effective Church Leadership: Building on the Twelve Keys.* San Francisco: Jossey-Bass/Wiley, 1990.

Carlson, Richard W. "Reflections on the Gift and Challenge of Vocation from Richard Carlson." Evangelical Covenant Church, Aug. 7, 2013. From *Covenant Companion*, May 1993. https://covchurch.org/2013/08/07/reflections-on-the-gift-and-challenge-of-vocation-from-richard-carlson/.

Center for Action and Contemplation. "The Edge of the Inside." Daily Meditations, Oct. 11, 2022. From Richard Rohr, "On the Edge of the Inside: The Prophetic Position," *Radical Grace* 25 (2012) 23–26. https://cac.org/daily-meditations/the-edge-of-the-inside-2022-10-11/.

Chandler, Russell. *Feeding the Flock: Restaurants and Churches You'd Stand in Line For.* Lanham, MD: Rowman & Littlefield, 1998.

Chbosky, Stephen, dir. *Nonnas.* Los Gatos, CA: Netflix, 2025.

Childress, Kyle. "Good Work: Learning About Ministry from Wendell Berry." *Christian Century,* Mar. 8, 2005. https://www.christiancentury.org/article/2005-03/good-work.

Clifton-Soderstrom, Michelle A. *Angels, Worms, and Bogeys: The Christian Ethic of Pietism.* Cascade Companions. Eugene, OR: Cascade, 2010.

Clinton, J. Robert. *The Making of a Leader: Recognizing the Lessons and Stages of Leadership Development.* Colorado Springs: NavPress, 1988.

Collier, Winn. "Holy Presence: Eugene Peterson's Pastoral Vision." Peterson Center for Christian Imagination, Mar. 19, 2021. https://petersoncenter.org/holy-presence-a-pastoral-vision/.

Collins, Jim. *Good to Great.* New York: Harper Business, 2001.

Conner, Benjamin T. *Practicing Witness: A Missional Vision of Christian Practices.* Grand Rapids: Eerdmans, 2011. Kindle.

Cormode, Scott. *The Innovative Church: How Leaders and Their Congregations Can Adapt in an Ever-Changing World.* Grand Rapids: Baker, 2020.

Creasy Dean, Kenda. *Almost Christian: What the Faith of Our Teenagers Is Telling the American Church.* New York: Oxford University Press, 2010.

Creech, R. Robert. *Family Systems and Congregational Life: A Map for Ministry.* Grand Rapids: Baker, 2019.

Daniel, Lillian. *This Odd and Wondrous Calling: The Public and Private Lives of Two Ministers.* Grand Rapids: Eerdmans, 2009.

Davey, Stephen. "Reconciliable Differences: Philippians 4:2–3; Extravangant Grace, Part 1." Wisdom Online, Mar. 6, 2016. https://www.wisdomonline.org/files/uploads/0003528ExtravagantGracePart1.pdf?srsltid=AfmBOoqk9m_6gx7nDFLX5DdDVDvgkH1K_BzZQTYDxkfZQJii6yADOGDp.

DeGroat, Chuck. *When Narcissism Comes to Church: Healing Your Community from Emotional and Spiritual Abuse.* Downers Grove, IL: IVP, 2020.

De Pree, Max. *Leadership Is an Art.* New York: Doubleday, 1989.

———. "What Is Leadership?" LeadershipNow, May 2024. From *Leadership Is an Art.* https://leadershipnow.com/Max_DePree_What_Is_Leadership.html.

De Pree Center Staff, The. "Upside Down Leadership: 10 Thought-Provoking Quotes from Max De Pree." De Pree Center, Oct. 25, 2024. https://depree.org/de-pree-journal/upside-down-leadership-10-thought-provoking-quotes-from-max-depree/.

DiMaggio, Paul J. "The Relevance of Organization Theory to the Study of Religion." In *Sacred Companies: Organizational Aspects of Religion and Religious Aspects of Organizations*, edited by N. J. Demerath III et al., 7–23. Religion in America. New York: Oxford University Press, 1998.

Donovan, Vincent J. *Christianity Rediscovered.* 25th anniv. ed. Maryknoll, NY: Orbis, 2003.

Drane, John. *The McDonaldization of the Church: Spirituality, Creativity, and the Future of the Church.* London: Darton, Longman, and Todd, 2000.

Drucker, Peter F. *The Post-Capitalist Society.* New York: HarperBusiness, 1993.

Duke Divinity School. "Traditioned Innovation Project." Duke Divinity School, n.d. https://divinity.duke.edu/initiatives/traditioned-innovation-project.

Dulles, Avery. *Models of the Church.* New York: Image, 2002.

Dunn, James D. G. *Acts of the Apostles*. Grand Rapids: Eerdmans, 1996.

Earls, Aaron. "Church Switchers Highlight Reasons for Congregational Change." Lifeway Research, Nov. 7, 2023. https://research.lifeway.com/2023/11/07/church-switchers-highlight-reasons-for-congregational-change/.

Edwards, Luke. "Lectio Vicinitas (Neighborhood Reading)." Central/Southern Illinois Synod, Evangelical Lutheran Church in America, 2019. https://www.csis-elca.org/wp-content/uploads/TLC-Lectio-Vicinitas.pdf.

Evangelical Covenant Church. *The Covenant Book of Worship*. Chicago: Covenant, 1986. Kindle.

———. "pH Check." Evangelical Covenant Church, n.d. https://phcheck.covchurch.org/.

Evans, Rachel Held. *Searching for Sunday: Loving, Leaving, and Finding the Church*. Nashville: Thomas Nelson, 2015.

Filz, Gretchen. "The Inspiring Prayer of St. Brendan the Navigator, Irish Patron of Sailors." Catholic Company, Feb. 2015; last updated May 16, 2017. https://www.catholiccompany.com/blogs/magazine/prayer-st-brendan-the-voyager-6061.

First Coast Churches. "Pastor Wellness Pathway." First Coast Churches, n.d. https://firstcoastchurches.com/pastor-wellness/.

Fitch, David E. *The Church of Us vs. Them: Freedom from a Faith That Feeds on Making Enemies*. Grand Rapids: Brazos, 2019.

———. *Faithful Presence: Seven Disciplines That Shape the Church for Mission*. Downers Grove, IL: IVP, 2016.

———. *Seven Practices for the Church on Mission: A Guide to Living What We Believe*. Downers Grove, IL: IVP, 2018.

Ford, Lance, et al. *The Starfish and the Spirit: Unleashing the Leadership Potential of Churches and Organizations*. Grand Rapids: Zondervan, 2021.

Foster, Richard J. *Celebration of Discipline: The Path to Spiritual Growth*. San Francisco: Harper & Row, 1978.

Fowler, James W. *Faith Development and Pastoral Care*. Nashville: Abingdon, 1987. Kindle.

Francis, Pope. *The Joy of the Gospel: Evangelii Gaudium*. Apostolic Exhortation. Vatican City: Vatican, 2013.

———. *With the Smell of the Sheep: The Pope Speaks to Priests, Bishops, and Other Shepherds*. Edited by Giuseppe Merola. Maryknoll, NY: Orbis, 2017. Kindle.

Franke, John R. *Missional Theology: An Introduction*. Grand Rapids: Baker Academic, 2020.

Fredrickson, Kurt. "The Church at Table: Being Sisters and Brothers Even When We Disagree." Fuller Studio, Oct. 6, 2020. From *Fuller Magazine* 18. https://fullerstudio.fuller.edu/theology/the-church-at-table-being-sisters-and-brothers-even-when-we-disagree.

———. "An Ecclesial Ecology for Denominational Futures: Nurturing Organic Structures for Missional Engagement." PhD diss., Fuller Theological Seminary, 2009.

———. "Let Us Cross Over to the Other Side." Fuller Studio, June 3, 2015. https://fullerstudio.fuller.edu/let-us-cross-over-to-the-other-side-kurt-fredrickson.

Frost, Michael. *Mission Is the Shape of Water: Learning From the Past to Inform Our Role in the World Today*. Cody, WY: 100 Movements, 2023. Kindle

———. *Surprise the World: The Five Habits of Highly Missional People*. Colorado Springs: NavPress, 2016.

Frost, Robert. "The Death of the Hired Man." Poetry Foundation, n.d. https://www.poetryfoundation.org/poems/44261/the-death-of-the-hired-man.

Fuellenbach, John. *Church: Community for the Kingdom*. American Society of Missiology. Maryknoll, NY: Orbis, 2002.

Galindo, Israel. *The Hidden Lives of Congregations: Discerning Church Dynamics*. Herndon, VA: Alban Institute, 2004.

Gehrz, Chris, and Mark Pattie III. *The Pietist Option: Hope for the Renewal of Christianity*. Downers Grove, IL: IVP Academic, 2017. Kindle.

Gerlach, Luther P., and Virginia H. Hine. *People, Power, Change: Movements of Social Transformation*. Indianapolis: Bobbs-Merrill, 1970.

Gibbons, Dave. *Small Cloud Rising: How Creatives, Dreamers, Poets, and Misfits Are Awakening the Ancient Future Church*. With Rob Wilkins. N.p.: Xealots, 2015.

Gibbs, Eddie. *The Rebirth of the Church: Applying Paul's Vision for Ministry in Our Post-Christian World*. Grand Rapids: Baker Academic, 2013.

Gibbs, Eddie, and Ryan K. Bolger. *Emerging Churches: Creating Christian Community in Postmodern Cultures*. Grand Rapids: Baker Academic, 2005.

Godin, Seth. *Tribes: We Need You to Lead Us*. New York: Penguin, 2008.

Gorman, Michael J. *Becoming the Gospel: Paul, Participation, and Mission*. The Gospel and Our Culture Series. Grand Rapids: Eerdmans, 2015.

———. *Cruciformity: Paul's Narrative Spirituality of the Cross*. Grand Rapids: Eerdmans, 2001.

Granberg-Michaelson, Wesley. *Unexpected Destinations: An Evangelical Pilgrimage to World Christianity*. Grand Rapids: Eerdmans, 2011. Kindle.

Green, Michael. *Evangelism in the Early Church: Lessons from the First Christians for the Church Today*. Grand Rapids: Eerdmans, 2003.

Grenz, Stanley J. *Renewing the Center: Evangelical Theology in a Post-Theological Era*. 2nd ed. Grand Rapids: Baker Academic, 2006.

Grenz, Stanley J., and John R. Franke. *Beyond Foundationalism: Shaping Theology in a Postmodern Context*. Louisville: Westminster John Knox, 2000.

Grothe, Daniel. *The Power of Place: Choosing Stability in a Rootless Age*. Nashville: Thomas Nelson, 2021.

Guder, Darrell L. "Missional Vocation: Called and Sent to Represent the Reign of God." In *Missional Church: A Vision for the Sending of the Church in North America*, edited by Darrell L. Guder, 1–17. The Gospel and Our Culture Series. Grand Rapids: Eerdmans, 1998.

———. "Walking Worthily: Missional Leadership after Christendom." *Princeton Seminary Bulletin* 28 (2007) 251–91.

Hall, Douglas John. "Ecclesia Crucis: The Disciple Community and the Future of the Church in North America." In *Theology and the Practice of Responsibility: Essays on Dietrich Bonhoeffer*, edited by Wayne Whitson Floyd Jr. and Charles Marsh, 59–76. Valley Forge, PA: Trinity, 1994.

Handley, Joseph W., Jr. *Polycentric Mission Leadership: Toward a New Theoretical Model for Global Leadership*. Regnum Studies in Mission. Minneapolis: Fortress, 2023.

Harvey, Barry. *Can These Bones Live? A Catholic Baptist Engagement with Ecclesiology, Hermeneutics, and Social Theory*. Grand Rapids: Brazos, 2008.

Hauerwas, Stanley. *The Peaceable Kingdom: A Primer in Christian Ethics*. Notre Dame, IN: University of Notre Dame Press, 1983.

Hauerwas, Stanley, and William H. Willimon. *The Holy Spirit*. Grand Rapids: Brazos, 2015.

Hayden, Josh. *Remissioning Church: A Field Guide to Bringing a Congregation Back to Life.* Downers Grove, IL: IVP, 2025.

Herrington, Jim, et al. *The Leader's Journey: Accepting the Call to Personal and Congregational Transformation.* Grand Rapids: Baker, 2003.

Hiebert, Paul G. "The Gospel in Our Culture: Methods of Social and Cultural Analysis." In *Church Between Gospel and Culture: The Emerging Mission in North America*, edited by George R. Hunsberger and Craig Van Gelder, 68–91. Grand Rapids: Eerdmans, 1996.

Hirsch, Alan. *5Q: Reactivating the Original Intelligence and Capacity of the Body of Christ.* [Cody, WY]: 100 Movements, 2017. Kindle.

———. *The Forgotten Ways: Reactivating the Missional Church.* Grand Rapids: Brazos, 2006.

Hirsch, Alan, and Tim Catchim. *The Permanent Revolution: Apostolic Imagination and Practice for the 21st Century Church.* With Mike Breen. Jossey-Bass Leadership Network Series. San Francisco: Jossey-Bass, 2012.

Hunsberger, George R. "The Newbigin Gauntlet: Developing a Domestic Missiology for North America." In *The Church Between Gospel and Culture: The Emerging Mission in North America*, edited by George R. Hunsberger and Craig Van Gelder, 3–25. Grand Rapids: Eerdmans, 1996.

Jennings, Willie James. *The Christian Imagination: Theology and the Origins of Race.* New Haven, CT: Yale University Press, 2010.

Jethani, Skye. *How Churches Became Cruise Ships: A Survival Guide for the Seasick Christian.* Downers Grove, IL: IVP, 2024.

Jones, L. Gregory, and Andrew P. Hogue. *Navigating the Future: Traditioned Innovation for Wilder Seas.* Nashville: Abingdon, 2021.

Jones, L. Gregory, and Kevin R. Armstrong. *Resurrecting Excellence: Shaping Faithful Christian Ministry.* Pulpit & Pew. Grand Rapids: Eerdmans, 2006. Kindle.

Kauffman, Stuart. *At Home in the Universe: The Search for the Laws of Self-Organization and Complexity.* New York: Oxford University Press, 1995.

Keefe-Perry, Callid. "Disturb Us, O Lord: The Misattributions and Authorship of a Prayer." Callid Keefe-Perry, Jan. 28, 2024. https://callidkeefeperry.com/the-image-of-fish/2024/1/28/disturb-us-o-lord-the-misattributions-and-authorship-of-a-prayer.

Kelly, Geffrey B., and F. Burton Nelson, eds. *Dietrich Bonhoeffer: A Testament to Freedom.* San Francisco: HarperCollins, 1995.

Kreider, Alan. *The Patient Ferment of the Early Church: The Improbable Rise of Christianity in the Roman Empire.* Grand Rapids: Baker Academic, 2016.

Küng, Hans. *The Church.* Translated by Ray Ockenden and Rosaleen Ockenden. New York: Sheed and Ward, 1967.

Langberg, Diane. *Redeeming Power: Understanding Authority and Abuse in the Church.* Grand Rapids: Brazos, 2020.

Leach, Tara Beth. *Radiant Church: Restoring the Credibility of Our Witness.* Downers Grove, IL: IVP, 2021.

Leader Breakthru. https://leaderbreakthru.com.

Lee, Cameron, and Kurt Fredrickson. *That Their Work Will Be a Joy: Understanding and Coping with the Challenges of Pastoral Ministry.* Eugene, OR: Cascade, 2012.

Lewis, C. S. *Mere Christianity.* New York: HarperCollins, 2001.

Love, Mark. "Competency Two: Discerning God's Calling in Communal Processes of Discernment." Dei-Liberations, n.d. Site discontinued.

Manning, Brennan. *Abba's Child: The Cry of the Heart for Intimate Belonging*. Colorado Springs: NavPress, 1994.

Marty, Peter W. "The Privilege of Ministry." *Christian Century*, Feb. 5, 2025. https://www.christiancentury.org/first-words/privilege-ministry.

McKnight, Scot. *A Fellowship of Differents: Showing the World God's Design for Life Together*. Grand Rapids: Zondervan, 2015.

———. *Pastor Paul: Nurturing a Culture of Christoformity in the Church*. Theological Explorations for the Church Catholic. Grand Rapids: Brazos, 2019.

McKnight, Scot, and Laura Barringer. *A Church Called Tov: Forming a Goodness Culture That Resists Abuses of Power and Promotes Healing*. Carol Stream, IL: Tyndale, 2020.

———. *Pivot: The Priorities, Practices, and Powers That Can Transform Your Church into a Tov Culture*. Carol Stream, IL: Tyndale, 2023.

McLaren, Brian D. *The Great Spiritual Migration: How the World's Largest Religion Is Seeking a Better Way to Be Christian*. New York: Convergent, 2016.

McNeal, Reggie. *Kingdom Come: Why We Must Give Up Our Obsession with Fixing the Church—and What We Should Do Instead*. Carol Stream, IL: Tyndale, 2015.

———. *Missional Renaissance: Changing the Scorecard for the Church*. Jossey-Bass Leadership Network Series. San Francisco: Jossey-Bass, 2009.

———. *A Work of Heart: Understanding How God Shapes Spiritual Leaders*. San Francisco: Jossey-Bass, 2000.

Meecham, Henry G. *The Epistle to Diognetus: The Greek Text with Introduction, Translation, and Notes*. Edited by Jacob N. Cerone. Classic Studies on the Apostolic Fathers. Eugene, OR: Pickwick, 2024.

Moltmann, Jürgen. *The Church in the Power of the Spirit: A Contribution to Messianic Ecclesiology*. Translated by Margaret Kohl. New York: Harper & Row, 1997.

Neuhaus, Richard John. *Freedom for Ministry*. Grand Rapids: Eerdmans, 1992.

Newbigin, Lesslie. *The Good Shepherd: Meditations on Christian Ministry in Today's World*. Grand Rapids: Eerdmans, 1977.

———. *The Gospel in a Pluralist Society*. Grand Rapids: Eerdmans, 1989.

———. *The Open Secret: An Introduction to the Theology of Mission*. Grand Rapids: Eerdmans, 1995.

Niebuhr, H. Richard. *The Purpose of the Church and Its Ministry: Reflections on the Aims of Theological Education in a Changing World Situation*. San Francisco: HarperCollins, 1983.

Nieuwhof, Carey. "How to Start a Ministry: 7 Missteps to Avoid." CareyNieuwhof.com, May 30, 2023. https://careynieuwhof.com/7-things-i-wish-someone-would-have-told-me-before-starting-ministry/.

Nouwen, Henri J. M. *In the Name of Jesus: Reflections on Christian Leadership*. New York: Crossroad, 1989.

———. *The Return of the Prodigal Son: A Story of Homecoming*. New York: Doubleday, 1992.

Oden, Thomas C. *Pastoral Theology: Essentials of Ministry*. San Francisco: HarperCollins, 1983.

Teresa of Ávila. "Christ Has No Body." Journey with Jesus, n.d. https://www.journeywithjesus.net/poemsandprayers/3637-Teresa_Of_Avila_Christ_Has_No_Body.

Tippett, Krista. "Brian McLaren: The Equation of Change." *On Being*, last updated Mar. 13, 2014. https://onbeing.org/programs/brian-mclaren-the-equation-of-change/.

Paas, Stefan. *Church Planting in the Secular West: Learning from the European Experience.* The Gospel and Our Culture Series. Grand Rapids: Eerdmans, 2016.

Packard, Josh. "Organizational Structure, Religious Belief, and Resistance: The Emerging Church." PhD diss., Vanderbilt University, 2008.

Pathak, Jay, and Dave Runyon. *The Art of Neighboring: Building Genuine Relationships Right Outside Your Door.* Grand Rapids: Baker, 2012.

Peace, Richard V. *Conversion in the New Testament: Paul and the Twelve.* Grand Rapids: Eerdmans, 1999.

Pemberton, Ryan. "Frederick Buechner on Calling: Your Deep Gladness & The World's Deep Hunger." Called, Dec. 22, 2014. https://www.calledthejourney.com/blog/2014/12/17/frederick-buechner-on-calling.

Peterson, Eugene. "'The Best Life': Eugene Peterson on Pastoral Ministry." *Christian Century*, Mar. 13, 2002. Interview by David Wood. https://www.christiancentury.org/article/2002-03/best-life.

———. *The Contemplative Pastor: Returning to the Art of Spiritual Direction.* Grand Rapids: Eerdmans, 1989.

———. "Faithful to the End: An Interview with Eugene Peterson." Religion News Service, Sept. 27, 2013. Interview by Jonathan Merritt. https://www.religionnews.com/2013/09/27/faithful-end-interview-eugene-peterson/.

———. *Leap Over a Wall: Earthy Spirituality for Everyday Christians.* San Francisco: HarperCollins, 1997.

———. *On Living Well: Brief Reflections on Wisdom for Walking in the Way of Jesus.* Edited by Winn Collier. Colorado Springs: WaterBrook, 2022.

———. *The Pastor: A Memoir.* New York: HarperOne, 2011.

———. "Pastoring Today—an Interview with Eugene Peterson." North American Baptist Conference, Sept. 7, 2016. Interview by Dan Hamil. https://nabconference.org/2016/09/pastoring-today-interview-eugene-peterson/.

———. *Practice Resurrection: A Conversation on Growing Up in Christ.* Grand Rapids: Eerdmans, 2010.

———. *Under the Unpredictable Plant: An Exploration in Vocational Holiness.* Grand Rapids: Eerdmans, 1994.

Pickard, Stephen. *Seeking the Church: An Introduction to Ecclesiology.* London, SCM, 2012.

Pietrzyk, Dan. "Shooting the Rapids: The Cycles of Pastoral Ministry." Faith & Leadership, Jan. 11, 2009. https://faithandleadership.com/shooting-the-rapids-the-cycles-pastoral-ministry.

Pohl, Christine D. *Making Room: Recovering Hospitality as a Christian Tradition.* Grand Rapids: Eerdmans, 1999. Kindle.

quoteresearch. "Quote Origin: Teach Them to Yearn for the Vast and Endless Sea." Quote Investigator, Aug. 25, 2025. https://quoteinvestigator.com/2015/08/25/sea/.

Rivers, Prince R. "The Witness of Hospitality." Alban at Duke Divinity School, May 16, 2025. https://alban.org/2025/05/16/the-witness-of-hospitality.

Rohr, Richard. *Everything Belongs: The Gift of Contemplative Prayer.* New York: Crossroad, 1999.

———. *Hope Against Darkness: The Transforming Vision of Saint Francis in an Age of Anxiety.* Cincinnati: St. Anthony Messenger, 2001.

———. *A Lever and a Place to Stand: The Contemplative Stance, the Active Prayer.* Mahwah, NJ: Paulist, 2011. Kindle.

Root, Andrew J., and Blair D. Bertrand. *When Church Stops Working: A Future for Your Congregation Beyond More Money, Programs, and Innovation*. Grand Rapids: Baker, 2023.

Roxburgh, Alan J. "Attend to What's Happening on the Ground." Faith & Leadership, Nov. 27, 2018. https://faithandleadership.com/alan-j-roxburgh-attend-whats-happening-the-ground.

———. *Joining God, Remaking Church, Changing the World: The New Shape of the Church in Our Time*. New York: Morehouse, 2015. Kindle.

———. *Missional: Joining God in the Neighborhood*. Allelon Missional Series. Grand Rapids: Baker, 2011.

———. "Missional Leadership: Equipping God's People for Mission." In *Missional Church: A Vision for the Sending of the Church in North America*, edited by Darrell L. Guder, 183–220.The Gospel and Our Culture Series. Grand Rapids: Eerdmans, 1998.

———. *The Missionary Congregation, Leadership, and Liminality*. Christian Mission & Modern Culture. Harrisburg, PA: Trinity, 1997.

———. *The Sky Is Falling: Leaders Lost in Transition*. Eagle, ID: ACI, 2005.

———. *Structured for Mission: Renewing the Culture of the Church*. Downers Grove, IL: IVP, 2015. Kindle.

Roxburgh, Alan J., and Fred Romanuk. *The Missional Leader: Equipping Your Church to Reach a Changing World*. Jossey-Bass Leadership Network Series. San Francisco: Jossey-Bass, 2006. Kindle.

Scazzero, Peter. *The Emotionally Healthy Leader: How Transforming Your Inner Life Will Deeply Transform Your Church, Team, and the World*. Grand Rapids: Zondervan, 2015.

Sechrest, Love L., et al., eds. *Can "White" People Be Saved? Triangulating Race, Theology, and Mission*. Missiological Engagements. Downers Grove, IL: IVP Academic, 2018.

Senkbeil, Harold L. *The Care of Souls: Cultivating a Pastor's Heart*. Bellingham, WA: Lexham, 2019.

Sevier County Baptist Association. "Pastor Wellness." Sevier County Baptist Association, n.d. https://www.sevbaptist.org/pastor-wellness.

Shenk, Wilbert R. "Mission, Renewal, and the Future of the Church." *International Bulletin of Missionary Research* 21 (1997) 154–59.

———. "New Wineskins for New Wine: Toward a Post-Christendom Ecclesiology." *International Bulletin of Missionary Research* 29 (2005) 73–79.

———. *Write the Vision: The Church Renewed*. Church Mission and Modern Culture. Eugene, OR: Wipf and Stock, 2001.

Shirky, Clay. *Cognitive Surplus: Creativity and Generosity in a Connected Age*. New York: Penguin, 2010.

Sine, Christine. "God Breathe on Us." In *Return To Our Senses: Reimagining How We Pray*, 14–15. Seattle: Mustard Seed, 2012.

Small, Kyle J. A. "Missional Ordered Ministry in the Evangelical Covenant Church: Moving Toward Apostolic Imagination." In *The Missional Church and Denominations: Helping Congregations Develop a Missional Identity*, edited by Craig Van Gelder, 198–234. Grand Rapids: Eerdmans, 2008.

Smith, C. Christopher. *How the Body of Christ Talks: Recovering the Practice of Conversation in the Church*. Grand Rapids: Brazos, 2019.

Smith, James K. A. *Introducing Radical Orthodoxy: Mapping a Post-Secular Theology*. Grand Rapids: Baker Academic, 2004.

Soerens, Tim. *Everywhere You Look: Discovering the Church Right Where You Are.* Downers Grove, IL: IVP, 2020.

Sorkin, Aaron. *The West Wing.* Season 1, episode 14, "Take This Sabbath Day." Directed by Thomas Schlamme. Aired Feb. 9, 2000, on NBC.

Sunquist, Scott W. *Understanding Christian Mission: Participation in Suffering and Glory.* Grand Rapids: Baker Academic, 2013.

———. *Why Church? A Basic Introduction.* Downers Grove, IL: IVP Academic, 2019. Kindle.

Sunquist, Scott W. and Amos Yong, eds. *The Gospel and Pluralism Today: Reassessing Lesslie Newbigin in the 21st Century.* Missiological Engagements. Downers Grove, IL: IVP Academic, 2015.

Swindoll, Charles R. *Rise and Shine: A Wake-Up Call.* Grand Rapids: Zondervan, 1989.

Thornburg, David D. *From the Campfire to the Holodeck: Creating Engaging and Powerful 21st-Century Learning Environments.* San Francisco: Jossey-Bass, 2014.

Tickle, Phyllis. *The Great Emergence: How Christianity Is Changing and Why.* Grand Rapids: Baker, 2008.

Tizon, Al. *Christ Among the Classes: The Rich, the Poor, and the Mission of the Church.* American Society of Missiology. Maryknoll, NY: Orbis, 2023.

Toffler, Alvin. *Future Shock.* New York: Random House, 1970.

Trueblood, Elton. *The Incendiary Fellowship: How the Church Can Be Set Aflame Today as It Was in the First Century of Christianity.* New York: Harper & Row, 1967.

Van Engen, Charles. *God's Missionary People: Rethinking the Purpose of the Local Church.* Grand Rapids: Baker Academic, 1991.

Van Gelder, Craig. *The Essence of the Church: A Community Created by the Spirit.* Repr., Grand Rapids: Baker, 2000.

———. *The Ministry of the Missional Church: A Community Led by the Spirit.* Grand Rapids: Baker, 2007.

———, ed. *The Missional Church and Denominations: Helping Congregations Develop a Missional Identity.* Grand Rapids: Eerdmans, 2008.

Van Gelder, Craig, and Dwight J. Zscheile. *The Missional Church in Perspective: Mapping Trends and Shaping the Conversation.* Missional Network. Grand Rapids: Baker Academic, 2011.

Vaters, Karl. *De-Sizing the Church: How Church Growth Became a Science, Then an Obsession, and What's Next.* Chicago: Moody, 2024.

Walling, Terry B. *Unlikely Nomads: In Search of the New Church.* Chico, CA: Leader BreakThru, 2023.

Watts, Isaac. "Joy to the World." Hymnary, 1719. https://hymnary.org/text/joy_to_the_world_the_lord_is_come.

Weborg, C. John. *Made Healthy in Ministry for Ministry.* Eugene, OR: Pickwick, 2011. Kindle.

Wheeler, Sondra Ely. *The Minister as Moral Theologian: Ethical Dimensions of Pastoral Leadership.* Grand Rapids: Baker Academic, 2017. Kindle.

Willard, Dallas. *The Divine Conspiracy: Rediscovering Our Hidden Life in God.* San Francisco: HarperCollins, 1998.

———. *The Great Omission: Reclaiming Jesus's Essential Teachings on Discipleship.* San Francisco: HarperCollins, 2006.

———. *Renovation of the Heart: Putting on the Character of Christ.* Colorado Springs: NavPress, 2002. Kindle.

———. *The Spirit of the Disciplines: Understanding How God Changes Lives*. San Francisco: HarperCollins, 1988.

Willimon, William H. *Calling and Character: Virtues of the Ordained Life*. Nashville: Abingdon, 2000.

———. *How Odd of God: Chosen for the Curious Vocation of Preaching*. Louisville: Westminster John Knox, 2015. Kindle.

———. *Pastor: The Theology and Practice of Ordained Leadership*. Nashville: Abingdon, 2002.

———. "Rev. Parker's Last Stand: Fifty Years of Preaching." *Christian Century*, May 4, 2004. https://www.christiancentury.org/article/2004-05/rev-parkers-last-stand.

Willimon, William H., and Stanley Hauerwas. "The Dangers of Providing Pastoral Care." *Christian Century*, Aug. 11, 2021. https://www.christiancentury.org/article/interview/dangers-providing-pastoral-care.

Winter, Ralph. "The Two Structures of God's Redemptive Mission." *Missiology* 2 (1974) 121–39.

Woodruff, Joel. "The Forgotten Letter 'D' for Discipleship." C. S. Lewis Institute, June 6, 2017. https://www.cslewisinstitute.org/resources/presidents-letter-the-forgotten-letter-d-for-discipleship/.

Woodward, JR. *Creating a Missional Culture*. Downers Grove, IL: IVP, 2012.

———. *The Scandal of Leadership*. Cody, WY: 100 Movements, 2023.

Wright, Christopher J. H. *The Mission of God: Unlocking the Bible's Grand Narrative*. Downers Grove, IL: IVP Academic, 2006.

Wytsma, Ken. *Myth of Equality: Uncovering the Roots of Injustice and Privilege*. Downers Grove, IL: IVP, 2017.

Yancey, Philip. *Church: Why Bother?* Grand Rapids: Zondervan, 1998.

Yang, Daniel, et al. *Becoming a Future-Ready Church: 8 Shifts to Encourage and Empower the Next Generation of Leaders*. Exponential Next. Grand Rapids: Zondervan, 2024. Kindle.

www.ingramcontent.com/pod-product-compliance
Lightning Source LLC
LaVergne TN
LVHW090518110826
845146LV00003B/904

* 9 7 9 8 3 8 5 2 4 0 0 9 8 *